BUSINESS ETHICS OF RETAIL EMPLOYEES

How Ethical Are Modern Workers? A Study of Morality based on Gender, Age, Education, and Management Experience

Bahaudin G. Mujtaba

ILEAD Academy, LLC
Davie, Florida. United States of America
www.ileadacademy.com

Bahaudin G. Mujtaba, 2010. *Business Ethics of Retail Employees: How Ethical Are Modern Workers?*

Cover Design by: Cagri Tanyar
Content Edits by: Lisa M. Mujtaba
Content Design by: Bahaudin G. Mujtaba

ISBN-10: 0-9774211-8-X

ISBN-13: 978-0-9774211-8-3

Subject Code & Description
  BUS008000 - Business & Economics: Business Ethics
  BUS057000 - Business & Economics: Industries - Retailing
  LAW036000 - Law: Ethics & Professional Responsibility
  PHI005000 - Philosophy: Ethics & Moral Philosophy

Printed in the United States of America by ILEAD Academy, LLC. Davie, Florida.

ILEAD ACADEMY
International
Leadership Education and Associate Development Academy

Dedication

This book is dedicated to my father Abagulim (Ghulam Mujtaba), who does what is right and in the right way in all circumstances. Thanks for being a great role-model!

June 30, 2009!

TABLE OF CONTENTS

PREFACE

The term *"ethical crises"* in the corporate world tends to be at the forefront of media discussions today amid a major economic recession in the United States. Some accuse business schools for not providing sufficient content on social responsibility and ethical decision-making, while others blame senior managers and leaders for choosing the wrong path in their decisions. While bankers, lenders, senior managers of the automotive industry, and politicians are often highlighted on a regular basis throughout various media outlets, retail employees and their ethical dilemmas are not necessarily always on the front page of major newspapers. However, retailers do come from the same cultures as others and are just as likely to have lapses in judgment since they too want to maximize shareholder values. Therefore, this study focuses on ethical perspectives of retail employees and managers.

Living in the days of unethical fiascos and debacles caused by people like Bernie Madoff and some senior managers at Enron, WorldCom, Tyco, and numerous others can easily symbolize human beings as animals who would do what they can to live and survive. However, some experts claim that a human being must be regarded as a social being whose development has been different from that of animals because of social relationships, cultures, and his or her concept of good and evil. This evolutionary advantage explains human development rather than genetic evolution, which is relatively slow; and it also lies at the origin of their enhanced capacity for adapting to his or her environment. Moral development theorists have been concluding that as human beings mature, that is grow older and gain more experience, their ethical values will tend to improve and they will become morally sophisticated. Theorists further conclude that this development can even take place as an individual reaches his or her thirties and forties. Researchers in human behavior also suggest that individuals develop their ethical values through their family life, school, religion, and other social influences. It must be stated that ethical sophistication and development requires learning from experience and case studies, because there are many difficult business ethical dilemmas which require prior training and familiarity.

In human beings, the social evolution has become more important than biological evolution, and has allowed rapid development. Some theorists also state that gender additionally accounts for differences in moral development because men and women see moral issues from different perspectives. Women are more caring and relationship-oriented; whereas, men are more predisposed toward justice and law.

This research uses Clark's (1966) instrument, which has been updated by Mujtaba (1997); Stephenson, Galbraith, and Grimm (1995);

as well as other researchers (Arlow and Ulrich, 1988; Stevens, 1984), to measure Personal Business Ethics Scores (PBES) of Supermarket managers and employees. The PBES measures personal commitment to integrity, honesty, and observance of the laws regulating current business activities. This research takes into consideration the respondents' age, supermarket management experience, education, and gender. This study contributes to the theory of moral development as it is tested in the Supermarket Industry for the first time. The results of this research suggest that age, supermarket management experience, and gender are factors which affect the moral development of supermarket associates and managers. Kohlberg's moral development theory is supported by this research.

All managers and workers are responsible for deepening their understanding of "right" and "wrong" conduct as they become employees of a corporation or in the public sector. This study shows that education and learning are factors in the moral development of individuals; and each person has the capacity to become morally sophisticated as he or she gets older and (presumably) becomes mature.

Since people are the common denominator of success and effectiveness, attaining progress and improvement are impossible ends with ineffective people as the means. The best way to promote fairness and cooperation, and to improve and empower people, is to educate and liberate all workers so they can take proper responsibility for their own choices in life, whether personal, professional, or business. One must become effective individually (privately and personally) before he/she can be effective with others, which is very important in this interdependent world. One must learn, not only how to create value for oneself, but also for others; and to do so in a legal, ethical, and socially responsible manner for all relevant stakeholders in the workplace.

This book provides an initial reflection and discussion on ethical development of retail workers for all human resource professionals, business students, managers, and employees in the workplace. Since this version of the research is prepared as a book, the citations and other resources are jointly listed in the bibliography for easier reading—for detailed citations and references, see the original dissertation research as follows:

Mujtaba, B. G., 1997. Business Ethics Survey of Supermarket Managers and Employees. UMI Dissertation Service. A Bell & Howell Company. UMI Number: 9717687. UMI: 300 North Zeeb Road. Ann Arbor, MI 48103. Phone: (313) 761-4700. (800) 521-0600.

Thank you for focusing on ethics and for reading this book.

ACKNOWLEDGEMENT

First, I would like to thank God for providing me the wisdom, motivation and ability to continue this type of research and education. Education is the common denominator of success for all human beings and I am certainly grateful, thankful and appreciative of this continued opportunity.

Second, I would like to thank my family members for believing in me and encouraging the best in me. I would like to especially thank my wife, Lisa Mujtaba, for her timely reviews, edits and suggestions in bringing this research to a closure. Thank you for being patient and supportive.

Third, I would like to thank my academic mentors and colleagues (especially Dr. Timothy O. McCartney, Dr. Frank J. Cavico, and Dr. Peter DiPaolo) for their valuable thoughts, step-by-step guidance, and warm support in the research process. This book is the product of my dissertation at Nova Southeastern University's H. Wayne Huizenga School of Business and Entrepreneurship and these fine faculty members and friends were excellent teachers, coaches and facilitators.

Finally, I would like to thank all of my professional colleagues in the retail environment for being flexible so I could attend school and continue this journey of progressively learning about life, morality and human nature. I would also like to thank you for reading this material on business ethics of retail workers. I wish you a life of integrity and value-creation for all humanity.

Thank you very much!

Bahaudin

1 – INTRODUCTION

Ethics and morality are at the core of discussion by people in most industries. This first chapter introduces the research focus and provides an overview of the book. It presents a brief background of the problem, purpose of the study, statement of the problem, significance of the study, and some of the terms used in this research. It presents assumptions, limitations, organization of the study, research questions, and working hypotheses.

Introduction and Research Problem

Many people are very concerned about the recent data which has documented the decline in moral behavior of senior managers in Corporate America today. As demonstrated from the cases of Enron, WorldCom, Tyco and others, respected and well paid executives and managers for example, are lying about company performance and using unethical practices, or they are pressuring their employees to lie for them. Business Week reports that contact lens managers, in order to beat sales targets, shipped products to distributors which were not ordered by them or the doctors. There are also serious ethical concerns distinguishing between "right" and "right," not merely "right" and "wrong." The traditional "right" goal of the firm has been to maximize shareholders' wealth; and thus moral issues currently are being viewed as a constraint on "profitable" behavior by the conventional financial economist. Doboson (1993) suggests that this view could cause people to act immorally. Others claim that the main purpose of a company should not be just to make a profit; but, rather it should be to make a profit in order to continue its business and to do so even better and more "abundantly."

Ethics education, morality and business ethics must be brought back into the planning process in order to build trust among all members of the firm. Trust generates commitment; commitment ensures effort; and efforts that are strategically positioned are necessary in today's competitive global economy (Hosmer, 1994).

Hosmer states that ethics and moral behavior should be central, not peripheral, to the overall management of the firm and its affairs. According to DeGeorge (1995), the point of business ethics is not to change peoples' moral convictions, but to build on them. He also states that morality should be at the core of the business because "morality is the oil as well as the glue of society and, therefore, of business" (p. 12). Ethical analysis is the only tool we can use to resolve conflicts in values and goals; and consequently is essential in the processes of corporate strategy throughout the world (Hosmer, 1994).

Despite the unethical conduct of so many senior managers and executives, researchers believe that older individuals, especially those who are managers and executives, possess a more strict view of moral issues than younger managers (Clark, 1966; Kohlberg, 1981/4; Arlow & Ulrich, 1980, 1985; Hallaq & Steinhorst, 1994; and Stephenson et al., 1995). According to Baumhart's (1961) study, in some business situations, executives, managers and their associates feel pressured to act immorally in order to save face and or their jobs. Baumhart found that younger managers were likely to compromise their personal principles in order to meet corporate and senior management expectations. Hallaq and Steinhorst (1994) stated that individuals with less work experience are more "hungry" for advancement opportunities and thus are more willing to accept marginally moral practices. There are other researchers who support the decline in business ethics, based on their interviews, questionnaires, and surveys which were conducted with business officials (Hosmer, 1988; Solomon, 1994; Wolfe, 1993; and Wallace, 1995).

If we would like to see better business ethics in our society, then we need to follow Gandhi's dictum of ethical integrity: "you must be the change you wish to see in the world" (Lichtenstein, Smith & Torbert, 1995). It has been proven that the central role of corporate leaders is to set the moral tone, culture, and standard for their organizations (Harris & Sutton, 1995).

Statement of the Problem

There have been many studies that link the moral and immoral behavior of individuals to their experience, age, gender, and maturity levels. Researchers (i.e., Kohlberg, Piaget, Clark) have concluded that as individuals mature (grow older and acquire experience), their ethical values and behaviors tend to improve. This growth in the moral development of individuals takes place from early childhood until the late twenties and early thirties. The "stage" theory of moral development states that people learn to think in a sequential mode, moving up the ladder of moral development one step at a time (Colby & Kohlberg, 1984). Colby and Kohlberg also concluded that individuals cannot skip a stage. They further state that this learning process can continue up to and beyond adolescence and early adulthood. They also define morally mature persons as those individuals who are in their late twenties or early thirties who possess a level of moral judgment and sophistication which cannot be found in adolescence.

Ruegger and King (1992) used questionnaires to test ethical behavior of students. They concluded that older students were more moral than younger students. Jadack, Hyde, Moore, and Keller (1995) completed a study of moral reasoning and concluded that older age groups had a significantly higher stage of moral reasoning than the younger age groups when responding to dilemmas about sexually transmitted diseases. Serwinek (1992) used questionnaires to survey insurance employees and concluded that older workers had stricter interpretations of moral/ethical standards than younger workers. It also has been shown that training and education on ethics can improve ethical standards and moral behaviors of individuals. For example, Beltramini (1984) distributed questionnaires to students and found that business majors were more concerned with ethical/moral issues than other majors.

The study of business ethics requires cooperation and understanding of everyones' opinions (Cooke, 1986). Cooke mentions that it is required that business people, academicians, ethicists, and government agencies combine their resources and gather answers for decision-making in business. It has been found that more and more of the top organizations are institutionalizing some type of ethical awareness programs in their companies (Nicholson, 1994). Research has shown that moral behavior was greater when companies had an organizational ethics policy or when companies provided ethics training for their employees. Models for managing moral/ethical behavior in business organizations are just beginning to be seen as a common denominator for much of an organization's objectives (Kotter & Hasket, 1992).

Researchers have concluded that moral/ethical values are related to the maturity (age) and experience/education. This study focuses on managers and non-managers to evaluate and examine their ethical values in relationship to their maturity levels and experience/education.

According to Hosmer (1994), moral standards differ between people; and the reasons are not clearly known. However, it seems apparent that there are religious/cultural and economic/social influences upon the development of moral standards (Jadack et al., 1995; Hosmer, 1994; and Kohlberg, 1981). A survey of business people concluded that older managers perceive themselves to be more ethical than younger managers (Hallaq & Steinhorst, 1994). Researchers also concluded that women also see themselves to be more ethical than men (Sikula & Costa, 1994). Many researchers agree that demographic variables such as age (Jadack et al., 1995) and gender do account for ethical differences (Liebert, 1984; Gilligan, 1982; Sikula & Costa, 1994).

Liebert (1984) states that differences in moral judgment level of individuals are caused by the level of information, knowledge, and experience which they have gone through. This level of moral maturity can take place in an individual's late twenties or early thirties as people enter the workforce and gain experience through the socialization process. Moral maturity, through practical experience, has been supported by the longitudinal study of Arlow and Ulrich (1985), where they reported that business people showed a greater level of moral sophistication ten years after completing an M.B.A. program than students who had recently completed their business degrees.

This study uses Clark's (1966) instrument to compare the results of Personal Business Ethics Scores (PBES) of Supermarket managers who have at least five years of management experience with Supermarket employees who are 25 years of age or younger and who have no formal management experience. The comparisons are based on age, management experience, education, and gender. The research question to be answered is whether age, gender, and management experience affect the moral development of individuals.

1. *Null Hypothesis I* - Individuals who are 25 years old or younger will have Personal Business Ethics Scores (PBES) that are equivalent to or greater than those individuals who are 26 years of age or older.

2. *Null Hypothesis II* - Females who are 25 years old or younger will have Personal Business Ethics Scores that are equivalent to or greater than males who are 25 years of age or younger.

3. *Null Hypothesis III* - Females who are 26 years of age or older will have Personal Business Ethics Scores that are equivalent to or greater than males who are 26 years of age or older.

4. *Null Hypothesis IV* - Individuals who have five or more years of supermarket management experience will have Personal Business Ethics Scores that are equivalent to or greater than individuals who do not have any management experience at all.

5. *Null Hypothesis V* - Females who have five or more years of supermarket management experience will have Personal Business Ethics Scores that are equivalent to or greater than males who have five or more years of supermarket management experience.

6. *Null Hypothesis VI* - Females with no management experience will have Personal Business Ethics Scores that are equivalent to or greater than males who have no management experience.

7. *Null Hypothesis VII* - Individuals who have four or more years of formal college education will have Personal Business Ethics Scores that are equivalent to or greater than individuals who do not have any formal college education.

Limitation of the Study

Ethical values of individuals are very personal; and thus their actions may vary depending on circumstances and other situational variables. People may say that they would act a certain way, but if they actually faced a moral issue, they might act differently. This notion has been supported by Smith, McGuire, Abbott, and Blau (1991), who suggested that what practitioners say they should do varies from what they actually would do. What they should do depends, to some degree, on formalized codes of ethics and authority figures; while what people would do is more related to non-codified guidelines, such as personal values and practical considerations of the situation.

Unfortunately, few people acknowledge their immoral acts; and this also is of some concern when examining how people respond to moral questions. Business ethics surveys which ask the participants only if they would do an action probably over estimates the ethical behavior of the sample (Cohen, Pant & Sharp, 1993). Not many people will respond that they would act immorally in prospective or hypothetical situations. Due to this problem, Clark (1966) has suggested that a means of finding out what people might do is to ask them if they approve or disapprove of a particular business decision. Clark (1966) created his instrument which uses scenarios. Respondents either approve or disapprove how each scenario has been decided. According to Clark, this method obtains the respondents' opinion on a particular matter, without putting him or her in a position of taking a moral stand. This research uses Clark's instrument to survey Supermarket managers and employees.

Significance of the Problem

A majority of researchers are calling for increased integration of ethical considerations into business ethics (Brown, 1994). Brown also concluded that business graduates are perceived to be ethically naive at best, and at worst, constrained in their moral development by the lack of ethical content in their courses. Cava (1990) suggested that a more productive way to start ethics education would be to find a way to stimulate critical thinking in decision-making.

Arlow and Ulrich (1980, 1984, 1988) used Clark's (1966) instrument and found differences in the responses of college business students based on their major field of study, and differences when compared to business managers. Stevens (1984) used Clark's instrument as well and surveyed 113 business executives and 349 business students. His results support previous researchers' (Clark, Arlow, Ulrich) findings that students had lower business ethics scores than business executives and managers. In a literature review of previous studies, no research was found that measured the ethical position of supermarket managers and supermarket employees.

In today's society, supermarkets are everywhere, and some families go there two to three times each week to purchase perishable and non-perishable products. Supermarket chains are constantly expanding in Florida; and this expansion creates opportunities for young people to move into management positions. The ethical position of these managers will affect their in-store sales, the company, as well as the local community. The majority of employees are part-time adolescents; and managers behavior and style of management can have a major impact on their moral behavior and development (Wimbush & Shepard, 1994).

Moral development theory suggests individuals learn to think in a sequential mode; and they move up and down the moral development stages without skipping or reverting to a prior stage (Kohlberg, 1984; Jadack et al., 1995). This research compares business ethics of supermarket managers who have five or more years of management experience with supermarket employees who do not have any management experience. Age, management experience, education, and gender are taken into consideration for this study of retail employees and managers.

Organization of the Study

This research is designed into five chapters. Chapter I presents the need for the study, statement of the problem and hypotheses, the limitation therein, and the significance of the study.

Chapter II is the literature review. It discusses the various ethical positions and concepts of philosophers as well as moral development theorists including Piaget, Kohlberg, Clark, Rest, and Gilligan, whose research have had remarkable impact on the subject.

Chapter III presents the methodology and the testing instrument. Clark's (1966) instrument has been chosen to test the ethical position of managers and non-managers in the supermarket industry. Many other researchers (Freedman, 1990; Arlow and Ulrich, 1980; and Stevens, 1984) have used this instrument because of its relevance to today's ethical dilemmas. These dilemmas include inflating expense accounts, falsifying records, promotion based on connections, illegal trades, conflicts of interests, and other similar morally questionable issues.

Chapter IV presents and interprets the collected data. Each Null Hypothesis is mentioned along with the results of the survey.

In Chapter V the results have been interpreted and analyzed to show the effects they may have on the supermarket industry. The findings are also compared with previous research which used Clark's instrument. This chapter also includes the summary, conclusions, biases in the research, and avenues of future research.

Summary

Ethics and morality are issues which are of critical importance for all employees, managers and leaders. This first chapter presented a brief background of the problem, purpose of the study, statement of the problem, significance of the study, and general concepts or terms. It presented organization of the study, research questions, and working hypotheses. This study uses a survey instrument to compare the results of Personal Business Ethics Scores (PBES) of supermarket managers who have at least five years of management experience with supermarket employees who are 25 years of age or younger and who have no formal management experience. The comparisons are based on age, management experience, education, and gender. The research question to be answered is *whether age, gender, education, and management experience impact the moral development of individuals.*

The next section, Chapter II, presents the literature review about ethics and each of the relevant variables. It discusses ethical concepts as well as moral development theorists whose studies have had remarkable impact over the past four decades.

CHAPTER TWO

II - LITERATURE REVIEW

Ethic is a subject that has been talked about since the beginning of time. Therefore, there is no shortage of content or literature about ethical theories or concepts. Chapter II is the literature review of relevant concepts related to the variables in this research. It discusses the various ethical positions and concepts of philosophers as well as moral development theorists including Piaget, Kohlberg, Clark, Rest, and Gilligan, whose research have had remarkable impact on the subject. It starts with the definitions of common terms and further provides specific citations related to age, gender, education, and management experience.

Introductory Definitions

Moral development theory states the people develop in their ethical maturity as they grow older and gain more experience in issues that deal with right and wrong, just and unjust, as well as good and bad. There are many dimensions and characteristics of a moral person. Often people confuse the term morality with ethics. Therefore, it is important to clarify some of the commonly used terms in this research.

Morality--is a system of conduct which is based on moral principles. In this case, moral relates to principles of right conduct and behavior; the behavior complies with accepted principles of what is considered right, just, and virtuous (according to Rich and DeVitis, 1994). Rich and DeVitis distinguish among morality, manners and mores. They relate manners with matters of taste and etiquette based on prudential judgments. Mores are related to the fixed morally-binding customs of a particular group; and mores vary to a great extent between different cultures.

There are two approaches to the study of morality: the scientific and the philosophical. The scientific approach uses the methodology of social and behavioral science to find out how people actually behave and what they believe about morality (Rich & DeVitis, 1994). The philosophical approach, however, is centered on ethics, which studies the nature of morality and moral acts. Ethics will be discussed later in this chapter.

Moral development--is the growth of an individual's ability to distinguish right from wrong, to develop a system of ethical values, and to learn to act morally (Rich and DeVitis, 1994). The term development refers to progressive and continuous changes from the beginning of life untill the end. As the research will show, moral development occurs through the process of not only maturity but socialization as well (Jadack et al., 1995). Kuper (1975) states that science, religion, culture, standards of good and bad, and other forms of behavior in society are passed on by nurture (that is, they are learned) and not by nature. Covey (1990) states that each individual has the ability to think about his or her very thought process, called "self-awareness." Covey further states that it is our "self-awareness" ability which enables us to make significant advances from generation to generation.

Socialization--is the process whereby individuals are becoming aware of societal values and acquiring appropriate social norms. This process is done by internalizing the social norms and guiding one's own actions to comply with the expectations of others.

Education--refers to an intentional process that has objectives, content, and outcomes; and can take place in a formal educational institution as well as other informal locations. Education differs from socialization, because education is designed to teach people new ideas and skills so as to improve their level of knowledge.

There are two motives or reasons for judgments (Rice, 1995). Firstly, there are objective judgments, which are based solely on the consequences of wrong-doing. Secondly, there are subjective judgments, which are judgments that take into account intention or motive. Rice says that children move from objective to subjective judgment as they become more responsible and when they deem motive or intention to be more important than consequences.

Moral Development

Moral character is an aspect of personality which may structure moral, ethical, and personal beliefs (Fritzche, 1995). In general, a person may be deemed moral when he/she behaves ethically. Moral behavior appears to be a function of one's past experience with similar situations (Fritzche, 1995) in which a person has learned to behave morally. Moral behavior is not "an inner entity operating independently of the situation in which individuals are placed" (Hemming, 1991).

Hemming (1991) states that social and moral potentialities may be nourished best through brain development between birth and maturity, supplemented by the process of education. Moral learning is not much different from any other form of learning since "moral learning is a matter of marrying-up, during the educational process, the potentiality for social relationships and behavior with the neural circuits that exist to sustain them" (Hemmings, 1991).

Society influences behavior of its members. For example, Kaltenheuser (1995) says that an Asian government is clearly and intentionally "stealing" Western technology to modernize its military and civilian industrial base. In most cases, this practice would seem fair and moral to the members of this Asian society, while in other societies this may be immoral.

Hemmings says that adolescence is the supreme socializing period and also that further moral development will take the form of "elaborating cerebral interconnections" which arise from a combination of motivation--the urge toward the fulfillment of potentialities--and learning. It is the interpersonal climate which is an important factor in the development of the moral function. There is evidence which suggests that intellectual stimulation also facilitates growth in moral judgment (Deemer & College, 1992). Deemer and College completed a study which neither find that individuals demonstrate growth in moral judgment regardless of experience, nor that, given certain experiences, all individuals develop. The human brain is full of resources for generating responsible, caring, civilized behavior, but, if these potentialities are to grow to maturity, one's social environment has to encourage this growth. All education is education of the brain; and moral education is not much different (Hemming, 1991). People with higher moral judgment scores are more likely to seek intellectual involvements. Also, people with high moral standards tend to go above and beyond the laws to make decisions that affect others (Savickas, 1995). It has been concluded that not everything immoral can be made illegal, because morality involves going above and beyond the written rules (Cavico, 1993). Cavico concludes that laws basically influence and shape moral standards, which reflect the moral beliefs of a society. The law plays a crucial role in ethical decisions, however, there is no guarantee that the law itself is ethical (Savickas, 1995); and, in some cases, meeting only the requirements of law might be considered unethical. In order to go above and beyond the call of duty, one faces different decisions which could be affected by his/her level of education, age, experience, and gender.

Education

There has been much research done to see if education affects moral maturity and behavior of individuals. Most of the researchers have concluded that education has a positive effect on the moral development of individuals. For example, Chap (1985) conducted a cross-sectional study of adult moral reasoning, comparing adults aged thirty-four to forty-nine with adults aged sixty-three to eighty-five years of age. Chap found that age and sex were not significant in relation to moral maturity scores on the Kohlberg measurements. He concluded that the results were supportive of the role of education in affecting moral reasoning. Walker (1986) completed a study of moral reasoning of adults between the ages of twenty three and eighty-four years of age. Based on his study, no participant reached stage four of moral reasoning without some college education. Most of the past research supports the fact that education helps individuals reach a higher level of moral development (Colby & Damon, 1992). Rest and Thoma (1986) used the Defining Issues Test and concluded that increased years of education were related positively to principled moral reasoning. White (1988) studied 195 subjects between ages of 19-82 years of age and reported that subjects who scored high on the moral reasoning test had more years of education than those who did not. Baxter and Rarick (1987) says that students would develop faster if moral development classes could be integrated or connected with the college or school curriculum. "The problem with education is to make the pupil see the wood by means of the trees" (Baxter & Rarick, 1987). They say that seeing the "connectedness" of things is the source of moral development. Life history makes a difference in that adult moral growth and development arise not from entertaining the logical possibility that one is wrong or fallible, but from actual experience of fallibility (Moody, 1994).

Gender

Most of the past research reports that gender does not affect the moral reasoning of individuals (Jadack et al., 1995; Pratt, Golding & Hunter, 1988). However, some researchers conclude that males and females pass through different stages of moral development at different age categories. Gilligan (1982) claims that while males are learning rules as part of their moral development, females are learning about intimacy, caring, helping, and relationships. Harris and Sutton (1995) completed a study comparing Fortune 1000 executives with MBA students and found that female MBA students' ethical judgment to be much closer to executives than male MBAs. They also found that female MBA students possess significantly different and less tolerant ethical values than male MBA students. Sikula and Costa (1994) found that men and women college students are ethically equivalent. However, males and females significantly differ on four other non-ethical values, which are an exciting life, a world at peace, forgiveness, and imagination. Compared to men, women students significantly value a world at peace and forgiveness more, and an exciting life and imagination less. White (1988) reported that sex was not itself a significant predictor of moral reasoning. The general feeling among the general public seems to be that females tend to make more moral decisions than men. Based on a study of college students, Sikula and Costa (1994) found that both men and women of today's youth (college age) have similar ethical and moral values; and they did not find any consistent, measurable differences between them.

Previous findings conclude that males and females can and do think of moral problems from different points of view, depending on the situation and context being considered (Fritzche, 1995; Jadack et al., 1995). Fritzche (1995) completed a study, which included 34 females and 66 males, and found that managers tend to respond to ethical dilemmas situationally, regardless of gender.

Age

Based on current literature, age will not improve one's moral maturity unless it is supported by education, training, and/or societal experiences. Just as one needs to be trained in learning a language, speaking and behaving politely, our cognitive thought process must be fed and challenged with moral issues, in order for moral maturity to take place. It also has been shown that feeding high fat diets to children can slow their cognitive development process (Elias, 1996). Perhaps living in an environment where unethical behavior is the norm can also make inappropriate choices more acceptable to individuals. Age can be a predictor of moral reasoning between individuals in different age categories (Jadack et al., 1995; Pratt, Golding & Hunter, 1988). White (1988) states that age is likely more predictive of children's moral reasoning than it is of adult reasoning, because the neurological-cognitive development which correlates with age in children acts to moderate the effects of environmental variables on moral reasoning and the confounding of age and education in children. For example, children between ages of 4-6 are more predictable than people who are between the ages of 40-70 years of age.

Children develop moral standards of their own; and these standards do not necessarily come from parents or peers but emerge from the cognitive interaction of children with their social environment. There is movement from one stage to the other that involves an internal cognitive reorganization rather than a simple acquisition of moral concepts, which are being practiced in their society (Kohlberg, 1984). Morality has been defined as a social institution composed of a set of standards that are pervasively acknowledged by the members of a culture (Beauchamp, 1988), and which must be learned by every young person during acculturation.

Although cognitive development is needed for the principles of moral reasoning, it does not guarantee, however, advanced moral development (Morris, 1982; Honeycutt, Siguaw & Hunt, 1995). Morris states that it is more useful to view moral development in terms of interactions between people's cognitive abilities and their experiences in the society.

Moral Development Researchers

Kohlberg's Stages of Moral Development

Kohlberg (1981, 1984) theorized that there are six distinct stages of moral development as seen in Figure 1; and movement along these stages normally occurs as a developmental progression, starting from somewhat immature to increasingly more complex and sophisticated levels of moral reasoning. Kohlberg describes moral development as a process of discovering universal moral principles, whereas Piaget (1975) understands moral development as a construction process (i.e., the interplay of action and thought builds moral concepts) (Kavathat-Zopoulos, 1991). Kohlberg presented individuals with hypothetical ethical dilemmas, asking what they would do in each situation, and then asking them to justify their choice of action. This is the procedure which he used to determine each individual's stage of moral development. The responses may not necessarily reflect a single stage, yet Kohlberg believed it was proper to characterize an individual as generally operating at a certain level/stage.

Kohlberg (1969, 1975, 1981, and 1984) created six stages of moral development which he categorized into three levels. The first level is called *Preconventional Morality* (concrete individual perspective) and the second level is called *Conventional Morality* (member of the society perspective), which leads to the third level called *Postconventional Morality* (prior-to-society perspective). Each level is divided into two stages and the movement from one level to next happens in orderly fashion without skipping a stage.

Stage one is the punishment and obedience orientation stage where everyone obeys all the rules in order to avoid punishment and the physical consequences of an action determine its goodness or badness. This is an egocentric point of view, where one does not consider the interests of others or recognize that they differ from the actor. Leadership that appeals to followers' self-interest is associated with this preconventional stage (Graham, 1995). One's actions are considered physically rather than in terms of the psychological interests of others. There is a confusion between authority's perspective and one's own views.

Figure 1 - Kohlberg's Moral Development Process

MORAL DEVELOPMENT STAGES

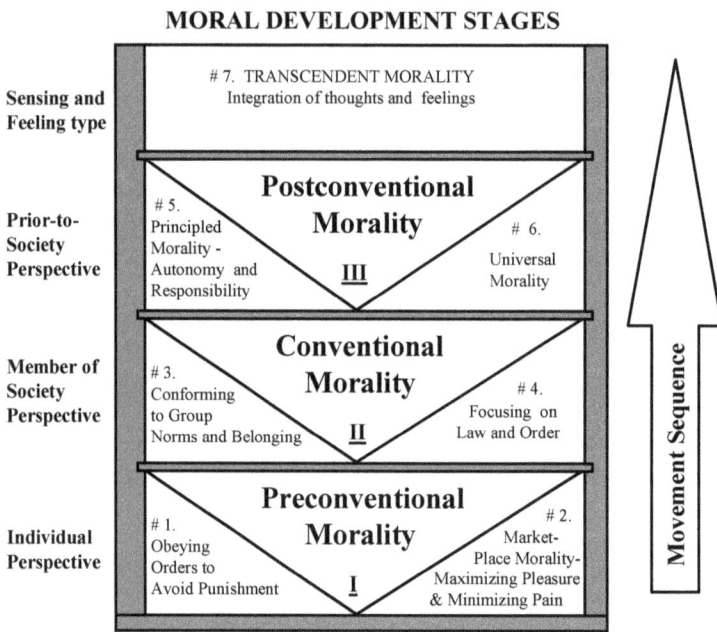

Kohlberg's Moral Development Stages: Stage 7 is defined by Gordon Shea (1988).

Stage two is the reward orientation; and, at this stage, individuals learn that doing the right thing will not only satisfy their own needs but will also occasionally satisfy the needs of others. Pragmatic, marketplace considerations determine right action (i.e., "you scratch my back and I'll scratch yours"). At this stage, maintaining or fulfilling the expectations of parents, group or organizational leader, and\or the nation is considered to be valuable, regardless of the immediate consequences, whether they are obvious or not. Individuals recognize that they have certain rights and accordingly others have the same rights or interests as well. One is aware that everyone has his or her own interest to pursue, demonstrating a concrete individualistic perspective.

At the third stage, the individual is trying to please others in order to avoid their disapproval; and this is referred as the "good boy" orientation, where the individual conforms to majority behavior. Being "nice" is the goal of the individual as it relates to the perception of those around him or her. The individual has a desire to maintain rules and authority which supports stereotypical "good" behavior. The perspective of the individual is determined in relationship to other individuals by putting himself or herself in other peoples' shoes.

The authority orientation is the fourth stage. Here, the individual upholds laws and social rules to avoid censure of authorities and feelings of guilt about not doing one's duty. Laws are upheld, except in extreme cases where they conflict with other fixed social duties. The individual feels obligated to meet his\her responsibilities because that is his\her given role in the system. According to Graham (1995), leadership styles of interpersonal relationships and social networks are associated with the conventional stages of moral development.

The next stage is the social-contract orientation, where the individual's own values and opinions enter into the moral decisions. The individual is aware of the relative nature of personal values and opinions; and determines behavior on the basis of social utility. At this stage, there is a clear effort to define moral values and principles that have validity and application regardless of the authority from the group or other leaders. The person feels obligated to make decisions that benefit the society as a whole, without considering opinions of others.

The final stage is the ethical principle orientation, where the individual chooses ethical principles and universal principles of equality and respect for the dignity of human beings. At this stage, right is defined as one's own conscience in accord with self-chosen ethical principles that are perceived to be the universal principles of justice. Consequently, a person may violate the law if it is not morally right and would follow the universal ethical principle of what should be done in such difficult situations.

The Postconventional Moral Perspective can be defined in terms of the individual's reasons why something is right or wrong. An individual at the Post-conventional level is aware of the moral point of view that a person in a moral conflict ought to adopt (Kohlberg, 1981). The Postconventional moral viewpoint recognizes fixed legal-social obligations and that moral obligations may take priority when the moral and legal viewpoints conflict.

The effects of exposure to Kohlberg's theory, particularly to description of the higher stages of moral judgment, have shown that subjects learn to make a favorable impression by learning the theory (Rest, 1986). Rest also states that exposure to the theory is a powerful educational tool for actually changing a person's moral thinking, except in cases where subjects are being post-tested. In such cases the exposure could contaminate the post-testing. Kohlberg found that working class children moved slower than the middle-class children in development (1981, 1984). This view has been supported by Havighurst (1994), who states that lower class youth feel less responsibility to the community and other social constraints because they did not participate in many social gatherings or community events.

Some researchers who have duplicated Kohlberg's study, have reported evidence that support the original results which states that the stages are fixed, sequential, and universal. While other researchers who have not been able to agree with Kohlberg's hypothesis, have given him credit for providing an avenue which has focused researchers to the study of cognitive and moral development.

Level IV (stage seven) has been suggested by Gordon Shea (1988). He believes that *transcendent morality* has long been in existence and we have little or no experience or research on it. Transcendent morality is based on integrity - integration of one's thoughts with one's feelings (creativity, caring, and sensitivity). Since, feelings and thoughts are not mutually exclusive, it can happen simultaneously. Gordon believes that more people will be striving for this stage and in time more people will achieve it.

Rest's Four Components of Inner Process

Rest and Narvaez (1994) developed four components of the inner process of moral behavior and they state that a person's moral behavior can be predicted if we know all four components of the inner processes. Rest and Narvaez (1994) claim that existing morality research can be organized according to this framework by involving one or more of these components.

At the first component, one sees the situation in terms of how one's actions affect the welfare of others. Then, he or she interprets the situation and identifies a moral problem (i.e., role-talking and determining how each situation is affected by various actions). Rest states that many people have a difficult time in interpreting even relatively simple situations, as shown by research on bystander reactions to emergencies. Research also shows that there are striking differences among individuals regarding their sensitivity to the needs and welfare of others (Rest, 1986). Rest also states that the ability to make judgments and inferences about the needs and wants of others is a "developmental phenomenon", that is, people improve in making inferences about others as they grow older. Some of the situational factors that influence the first component are the time allowed for interpretation, familiarity with people involved or the situation, and the ambiguity of people's needs, intentions, and actions.

At the second component, individuals decide what the moral courses of actions would be in each situation by involving the concepts of fairness and justice, moral judgment, and application of social-moral norms. First of all, social psychology postulates that social norms govern how a moral course of action is to be defined (Rest, 1984). One of the social norms is social responsibility. For example, if you see a person that needs your help and this person is dependent on you, then you should help this person. Secondly, there is the cognitive-development approach, which focuses on the progressive understanding of the purpose. The focus here is to establish cooperative arrangements and reveal how the participants are benefiting from this cooperation. Influences in this component are factors affecting the application of particular social norms or moral ideals, or their activation, delegation of responsibility to someone else, the particular combinations of moral issues involved, and prior conditions, contracts, and commitments (Rest, 1984).

At the third component, the individual chooses a course of action from many alternatives and decides if he/she will fulfill his/her moral ideals. In this stage, there could be many different alternatives, some of which could be influenced by strong and attractive non-moral values that might make a person choose a course of action which compromises his or her moral ideal (Rest, 1986). Rest also states that people make moral decisions because:

- Evolution has bred altruism into their genetic inheritance;
- There is no special motivation to be moral; people just respond to reinforcement or modeling opportunities and learn social behavior; and
- Conscience makes cowards of us all, that is, shame, guilt, conditioned negative effects, and fear of God, motivate morality as well.

Influences on these components are factors that activate different motives, other than moral motives, which may include mood states which influence decision making, costs and benefits, probability of certain occurrences, and factors that affect one's self-esteem and willingness of associated risk-taking.

The final component is the execution and implementation of the individual's intentions. This involves determining the proper courses of action, following through to make sure everything is going as planned and overcoming unexpected difficulties while keeping in focus the end result. It has been suggested that certain inner strength, and an ability to mobilize oneself to action, play an important role in production of moral behavior. Some of the influential factors in this component are factors that physically prevent one from carrying out a moral plan of action, cognitive transformations of the goal, and timing difficulties in managing more than one can plan at a time.

Rest states that even though there is a logical sequentiality to the four components, they are interactive and thus not proposed as a linear decision-making model. He also states that individuals go through two stages while making moral judgments in real situations. Firstly, the person recognizes what is the right action in the particular situation, and then he/she judges his/her own responsibility in the situation to perform the right action and get it done.

Piaget's Stages of Moral Development

Jean Piaget (1975) has done much research in the area of children's intellectual or cognitive moral development by studying the structure of their growth. Piaget was trained as a zoologist and saw all behaviors in terms of a person's adaptation to the environment (Morris, 1982). A study, completed at the University of Maryland's School of Medicine in Baltimore, concluded that the more fat and calories children eat, the more potentially harmful lead there is in their blood (Elias, 1996). It has been found that excess lead impairs children's cognitive development. Piaget has established a continuum of cognitive moral development which consists of four stages. Children develop along these four stages without going back to a lower stage (Piaget, 1975).

Piaget's first stage is called the *Sensory-Motor Stage* and it deals with motor and individual characteristics of the child, who learns about him/her-self and the environments around him/her. Children go through this stage at about the age of two. At the end of the sensory-motor stage, children develop a sense of object permanence. When the baby begins to look for a ball that has rolled under a chair, we can conclude that the child realizes that the ball still exists. By the end of this stage, children also have a sense of self-recognition.

The second stage is called *Preoperational Thought Stage*, where children are action-oriented and egocentric (that is, at this stage they cannot put themselves in someone else's place). The child learns the rules of behavior; and in some cases they make-up the rules until they gain familiarity with the rules. Children pass through this stage between the ages of two to five years old. The child's ability to remember and anticipate grows; and, it is at this stage, that they learn to use words to describe objects. Piaget also has suggested that children in the preoperational stage have a tendency to focus on one aspect of the situation and ignore all the others.

At the third stage, called *Concrete Operation*, children become more flexible than they were at the preoperational stage. They learn to retrace their thoughts, correct themselves, and start over if necessary. They can look at a single object from different points of view. They learn to cooperate, because the rules seem to be very vague, and they may agree to change them at any time. This stage occurs between the children of seven to eleven years old.

The fourth stage is called the *Formal Operations*, which is the codification, where all the rules are known and fixed. This occurs during the adolescence at 11 to 15 years of age (at time of discovery and experimentation). It is in adolescence that people realize how the fact of being born into a particular culture has influenced their values, opportunities, and personalities (Morris, 1982). Young children solve complex problems by testing their ideas in the real world; their explanations are concrete and specific. They can understand things in terms of cause and effect; and they can consider the possibilities as well as the realities. The cognitive changes that occur during this stage make people more aware of the gap between the real and the ideal. Realizing this may lead to a personal goal--a commitment to close the gap and the perception of not being able to close this gap may lead to depression and rebellion (Morris, 1982).

Piaget's data shows that very young children tend to judge the naughtiness or wrongness of the behavior solely on the basis of consequences (Piaget, 1975). He has inferred that group discussions and training adults in moral/ethical decision making processes can influence an individual's reasoning process. Paradise (1977) concluded that subjects who were involved in group discussions involving ethical reasoning at the "principle level" of ethical judgment, tended to score higher on the Ethical Judgment Scale than subjects who were not exposed to such discussions. So, adults can learn similar to children, but the development of their moral values may take more time, effort and an encouraging environment to figure out the consequences.

Liebert's Moral Sophistication Theory

Liebert (1984) states that according to the cognitive-behavioral view, moral sophistication is what develops in moral development. Moral sophistication is the general term for knowing how to pursue one's own long-term self-interest effectively, either directly or indirectly. As a result of this interplay of cognitive development and social experience, people accomplish a grasp of both the direct and immediate as well as the indirect and long-term effects of their words and deeds. The result is a new level of practical understanding which, in turn, can determine what we say and do. According to Liebert (1984):

> Moral development is a matter of learning what the moral standards and norms of one's society are, of determining how and when they are applied, including by whom, to whom, and with which short-term and long-term consequences. (p. 184)

Liebert explains the inconsistencies in moral reasoning and personal conduct, in that the actual situation, and not moral principles, dictate individual moral judgments. Liebert also states that there is not much doubt that the moral justifications offered by people are related to age, gender, IQ, demographic variables, and social class. The relationship between these variables reflect information, knowledge, and experience differentials which are possessed by various groups of people rather than differences in their understanding of what is good or bad.

Liebert (1984) states that ethical philosophers have not supported Kohlberg's universality of moral principles and the empirical studies do not support the three-level (six stage) theory of moral development. According to Liebert (1984) and DeGeorge (1995), research has shown that standards and values as to what is good, moral, or right vary widely from one culture to another. "The substance of human moral belief seems to share no moral precept that could be called universal" (Liebert, 1984).

Colby and Kohlberg's Research

Kohlberg has hypothesized that his developmental levels constitute stages in strict Piagetian sense. Firstly, the stage concept implies that under normal environmental conditions the development will always be in an upward direction. Secondly, individuals will go through each stage without skipping a stage. Thirdly, the stage concept implies that individual thinking will be at a single dominant stage across varying content, although to some degree, overlap of the adjacent stage may be expected.

Colby and Kohlberg's (1984) findings are based on a 20 year longitudinal study of 53 males. Based on this study, they stated that moral development of young adults extended to their late twenties and thirties. For years, psychologist accepted what now seems an incredible notion: that development starts prenatally and stops as people reach adolescence. Rice (1995) states that emotional maturation continues along with the socialization process throughout one's life. He further states that some measures of intelligence indicate that cognitive development continues past the age of sixty.

Colby and Kohlberg (1984) stated that true stage five does not occur until an individual is well into his\her twenties or thirties. This also explains why 30 year-olds seem to be more sophisticated in their judgments than adolescents and teenagers. They conclude, therefore, that age is a variable in making moral decisions and learning can continue as we grow and gain more experience.

Gilligan's Theory of Moral Development

Carol Gilligan has agreed with Freud's claim that "for women the level of what is ethically normal is different from what it is in men" (Crittenden, 1990). She has challenged Kohlberg's theories in light of her own research on women. According to Rich and DeVitis (1994), Gilligan's thesis puts emphasis on a language of care, responsibility and not wanting to hurt others in women's presumably unique moral vision.

According to Gilligan (1982), men and women speak in different voices. She argues that there are biases in Kohlberg's scoring methods because they were mainly constructed for male subjects. In Kohlberg's scoring method, the average adolescent female attained a rating which corresponds to type 3 ("good boy" and "nice girl" orientation), while the average adolescent male attained a rating corresponding to type 4 ("law-and-order" orientation).

Gilligan (1982) found that females approach moral issues from different perspectives than men. Women emphasize sensitivity to others' feelings and rights, and show concern and care for others. Men, however, emphasize justice-preserving principles, rules, and rights. She states that women rely on an interpersonal network of care orientation, and men rely more heavily on justice orientation. She states that if women have a predominant care orientation and men have a predominant justice orientation, then Kohlberg's test would produce different results in favor of the men.

Because of the difference in the way men and women think, Gilligan proposed a female alternative to Kohlberg's stages of moral reasoning. This theory is similar to Kohlberg's, as it emphasizes that the development of moral judgment is a gradual cognitive process, stimulated by increasing, changing, social relationships of children as they get older.

At Level I (Preconventional Morality), women are concerned with survival and self-interest. Eventually, they realize the difference between their selfishness and what they ought to be doing (responsibility).

At Level II (Conventional Morality), women start sacrificing their own preferences in order to become responsible and caring for others.

At Level III (Postconventional Morality), women develop a universal perspective, where they become concerned about the consequences for all, including themselves, in making decisions.

Havighurst's Developmental Tasks Research

According to Havighurst (1994), the developmental task stage takes place at a certain period in an individual's life. If an individual completes this developmental task, then this experience could lead this person to much more success in achieving the future tasks and happiness. Failure to complete the developmental task successfully, however, could lead to unhappiness, difficulty with later tasks, and disapproval by the society in general.

Havighurst (1994) has proposed ten developmental tasks for adolescence; and the two developmental tasks that directly relate to moral development are as follows: first, desiring and achieving socially responsible behavior; and secondly, acquiring a set of values and an ethical system as a guide to behavior. These tasks should be accomplished at a proper time; and failure of this could cause partial or complete failure in subsequent tasks.

Havighurst has suggested that achieving the developmental tasks depends on psychological and cultural variables in the society. In other words, it is a learned behavior which is influenced by the society and its cultural norms. It is important to provide the conditions to facilitate appropriate task achievements. Psychologically, the adolescent learns to make sacrifices for the greater good of the family or society, and as a result, this individual could be rewarded for acting appropriately or showing the desired behavior.

It is important for adolescents to participate in social gatherings and community affairs because this advancement can help them become altruistic and consider the larger social good (Havighust, 1994). Unfortunately, many lower and middle class youth do not get the chance to participate in social and community affairs because they leave for college, work or cannot afford them. So, they feel less responsibility to the society and community in general. He suggests that schools, secondary for adolescence, can teach about the life of the local community in the studies of economic and social relations. By doing this, we can promote developmental task as we are providing the conditions to facilitate appropriate task achievements.

Havighurst holds that values form a hierarchy; and physiological drives are the primary sources of all values. The adolescent learns the appropriate values in six ways: satisfaction of physiological drives, fulfillment of emotional experiences, consistent reward and punishments, association of the desired value with love or approval, inculcation by an authority figure, and reasoning as well as reflective thinking. He concludes by stating that adolescents learn from role models, peers, family, and society in general. Proper adult supervision therefore is needed in order to help adolescents acquire desired values.

A longitudinal study conducted by Peek and Havighurst (1962) produced similar results. The authors concluded that the actions of role models in home (parents, brothers, sisters, and other family members) are of great importance to the child's development. Peek and Harvighurst estimate that almost 25% of the population is at the highest level of moral development. These individuals assess each new action in terms of internalized moral principles accumulated through social experiences, and they are honest, dependable and act on what is morally right.

Peek and Havighurst concluded that adolescents learn based on what the family, peers, and society expect from them. This expectation helps them to conduct themselves appropriately in order to support their well-being and build on their moral development process which can continue into even middle ages at which point these individuals are considered to be morally sophisticated.

Torbert's Research on Moral Development Stages

Torbert (1991) has stated that successive stages of personal development have an ethical logic which closely parallels the socio-historical development of ethical philosophies during the modern era. He supports past research which concluded that each sequential ethical theory explicitly outlines a coherent world view held implicitly by persons at successively late development stages. Because each higher developmental stage includes cumulative abilities and distinctions of all the earlier stages, individuals at the higher stages are capable of making more sophisticated ethical judgments that are responsive to more elements of a given situation or dilemma (Lichtenstein, Smith & Torbert, 1995). Lichtenstein, Smith, and Torbert (1995) concluded that individuals at the later stages of developmental theory are more ethical than those in previous stages.

Torbert has created a model of developmental theory which has eight stages and the progress is similar to Kohlberg's model, utilizing a sequential mode without skipping a stage. He has proposed eight stages and they are impulsive, opportunist, diplomat, technician, achiever, strategist, magician, and ironist. Based on interviews with about 500 managers, no one has fallen in the impulsive stage, and majority of the managers fall in the technician category.

Opportunists usually focus on tangible symbols of power. They are often deceptive and distrustful, and they seek to get away with anything they can. Diplomat category individuals would seek status and approval from their immediate group; and their loyalty is to their immediate group as well. They understand the rights and social norms of the society and the people. The technicians treat people as technical systems, and they often seek to stand out and be unique. They usually try to do things "the right way." Achievers appreciate complexity and seek mutuality in relationships. They strive for excellence and self-set standards.

Strategists try to get things done in a systematic fashion, yet they value other perspectives, and see their own and other perspectives to be flexible and modifiable. Only 10% of the managers sampled fell into this category. From the sample of 500 managers, no one was categorized in the magician or the ironist stages. Magicians and ironists are similar to Kohlberg's universal and natural law stages. People in these stages usually would be engaged in public inquiry actions, with the goal of exercising vulnerable, mutually transforming, power (Torbert, 1991).

Torbert's last three stages of managerial development have been considered to be the late-stages: the Strategist, the Magician, and the Ironist. He considers these stages to be post-formal individuals who at this level develop their own system of ethics through their interactions with varying environmental contexts, rather than by adopting the traditional or formal philosophies drawn from the society or an institution.

Philosophical Ethics and Definitions
The economy can change for better or worse depending on what people in that economy choose to do, and what people choose to do is greatly influenced by their respective ethics (Takala & Uusitalo, 1995). They further state that the majority of people want a just or good society. However, Lee and McKenzie (1995) state that business people are not always as honest as we would like them to be, but they are more honest than perceive. They also mention that it would foolish to assume all business people are honest and trustworthy.

Peter Drucker (1994) states that ethics is not a new or recent discovery; philosophers, over centuries, have struggled with human behavior to develop different approaches to ethics, many resulting in different conclusions and conflicting rules of behavior. Shea (1988), Shaw and Barry (1992), and Wood (1990) state that ethics involves the discipline of dealing with what is right or wrong with moral duty and obligation. Ethics determines the guidelines for right and wrong behaviors, and the new view of management holds that ethics is essential in business (Collins, 1994). Moral judgements concerning ethical behavior of people are made by the society, as well as business leaders (Gellerman, 1986). Shaw and Barry state that the word "ethic" comes from the Greek word "ethos," meaning character or custom. The "ethos" is used to distinguish disposition, character, or attitude of a specific culture or group. The universal principle of ethics is to act always in such away that everyone else faced with the same situation would take the same position (Hosmer, 1994). Dean (1992) states that if people are given the skills and examples that will enable them to make better decisions, then they can apply them to any situation consistently based on universalism (Kant) principle.

According to Solomon (1994), ethics is basically concerned with individual character, including what it means to be a "good person" and the social rules that govern and limit one's conduct, especially the ultimate rules concerning right and wrong, which are referred to as morality. One can distinguish between morality and ethics by stating that morality refers to human conducts and values, where as ethics refers to the study of human conduct and values (Shaw & Barry, 1992). However, the words "unethical" and "immoral" seem to have been used interchangeably describing actions or behaviors that do not meet desired standards. On the other hand the words "ethical" and "moral" have been used to describe a desirable standard of behavior or performance (DeGeorge, 1995).

We can define ethical behavior as doing the right thing; however, the problem arises in the definition of doing the right thing. Everyone has his/her own opinions and judgments on what the right thing is, and that is what creates the problem (Richter & Barnum, 1994). For the purpose of this study, doing the right thing will be defined as abiding by publicly enunciated ethically determined rules, where the majority of the people will see a decision as a moral decision. Individuals by rationalization can "justify" their actions, but the public may not see it as just or moral.

Webster's definition of ethical is "the philosophy of distinction between right and wrong and moral duty and obligation to the community." Ethically motivated behavior would mean the actual performance of such distinctions and obligations, and not just merely being aware of its existence. It is the moral behavior of individuals that gets results and creates an effective and motivational organizational culture. By simply having an organizational code of conduct, we are merely wasting paper and precious time because it is the actual implementation and training which creates moral results (Harris & Sutton, 1995).

According to DeGeorge (1995), ethics is the study of morality; and it concerns itself with human conduct or activity that is done knowingly and willingly. DeGeorge states that the term "ethics" is used in a variety of ways by different philosophers and researchers. However, the three common areas of ethics are: descriptive ethics, normative ethics, and metaethics.

Descriptive ethics is related to anthropology, psychology, and sociology. It describes the morality of people, society, and culture. Normative ethics builds on descriptive ethics and attempts to supply and justify a coherent moral system based on it. It deals with the issues of goodness or badness and rightness or wrongness of subjects/actions that moral philosophers study. Metaethics is the study of normative ethics; and to some extent metaethical activity is involved in both normative and descriptive ethics. Metaethics tries to find out the meaning of goodness or badness and rightness or wrongness.

Two popular principles of ethics are teleology and deontology (Harris & Sutton, 1995). Teleology deals with the consequences and results of an action, where good results are considered morally right and bad outcomes are considered morally wrong. Teleology is divided into egoism, where an individual seeks the best long-term self-interest for him or herself; and utilitarianism, where the moral actions are based on the greatest benefits to greatest number of people. Deontology deals with the reason of why an act is performed and whether it was performed for the right reason (Harris & Sutton, 1995). Deontology claims we should not judge actions based on their consequences, but because they are morally right or wrong in and of themselves. The deontologist claims that actions are right or wrong independent of their consequences (DeGeorge, 1995).

Sims (1994) describes three ethical positions that can provide guidance to people in business for evaluating their own ethical standards. They are utilitarianism, rights, and justice.

Utilitarianism

The first theory is the utilitarian view of ethics, where decisions are made based on the consequences of each action (Harris & Sutton, 1995). The goal of the utilitarian is to provide the greatest good for the largest number of people or groups (Cavanagh, Moberg & Velasquez, 1995). This theory seeks to provide an objective means for making a moral decision (Wood, 1990). This theory basically states a formula, where the outcome, or net benefit, is produced as a result of the consequences of actions or decisions. Therefore, an action is morally right, if and only if, the sum total utility produced is greater than the alternative actions (Harris & Sutton, 1995). Based on this theory, a corporation is obliged to do not that which will produce the largest benefit to itself, but that which will have a greater positive impact on all of the corporation's stakeholders, including the society at large (Wood, 1990).

While the utilitarian view promotes efficiency and productivity, it can still result in ignoring the rights of some individuals, especially those who form the minority sector of the organization (1994, Sims). Another problem with the application of utilitarian theory is the measurement of utility. It is very difficult to assign a common instrument to measure utility, because people do not value outcomes in the same way and the value of each outcome could vary depending on time, culture, and situation (Wood, 1990).

Rights

This view of ethics expects individuals to make decisions which are consistent with fundamental liberties and privileges as set forth in documents like the Bill of Rights (Cavanagh, Moberg & Velasquez, 1995). As Stoner and Freeman (1988) state: a "right" is a claim which entitles a person to the "room" in which to take action. The term "room" could be referred to as a person's "sphere of autonomy" or simply one's freedom. "Rights" not only permit individuals to have a free and equal choice in pursuing their interest, but "rights" also serve as a justification for one's behavior. The "right" perspective protects individuals from injury, and is consistent with freedom and privacy, however, it can create an overly legalistic work environment which could interfere with productivity and efficiency (Sims, 1994).

Justice

The third ethical perspective requires individuals to impose and enforce rules fairly and impartially so there is an equitable distribution of benefits and costs (Sims, 1994; Cavanagh, Moberg & Velasquez, 1995). This view is consistent with that of unions' demands for paying people the same wage and using seniority as a standard. Justice and fairness are concerned with the comparative treatment given to members of group or society when benefits and costs are distributed (Shefrin & Statman, 1993).

DeGeorge (1995) mentions four different kinds of justice. *Compensatory* justice is concerned with fairness of victims' compensation particularly as to whether it is equal to a victim's loss. *Retributive* justice concerns itself with the fairness of how the rule-breakers are identified and punished; and the process of how these sanctions are applied. *Procedural* justice is a term which is used to designate fair decision-making procedures, practices, or agreements. *Distributive* justice is concerned with how fairly the benefits and burdens are distributed in a society (Shefrin & Statman, 1993).

DeGeorge (1995) also mentions that ethics is an independent subset of philosophy which studies the moral principles of individuals and societies. Ethics deals with the rules that should govern human conduct and the values which people desire to pursue. He further states that there are many ethical considerations in today's competitive environment of business. As managers and business leaders, we should encourage everyone to deal with each situation fairly and honestly so as to create an environment where each person has equal opportunity.

Business Ethics

Nash (1994) paraphrases Mark Twain and states: "...reader, suppose you are a businessman. Now suppose you are of ruthless and greedy character. But I repeat myself." Nash states that these kinds of statements about business executives have appeared in the popular press, which states the truth about the immoral acts that people are committing throughout all functions of business.

Ethics in America seem to have dropped to one of the lowest points in history (Wood, 1990), and it appears in the media as one of the pressing issues of the modern times (Dean, 1992) and today's concerns (Neubaum, Pagell, Drexler, McKee-Ryan, and Larson, 2009). Some critics claim that business schools focus too much on the achievement of tasks at all costs and that this indoctrination has led to unethical behaviors and scandals associated with Enron, Tyco, WorldCom, and other such firms (Mitroff, 2004; Ghoshal, 2005). According to Neubaum, Pagell, Drexler, McKee-Ryan, and Larson (2009), "many of the recent discussions of business schools have centered not on the good their graduates do, but on how the theoretical foundations of business school education may be linked to ethical lapses and scandals involving managers who have been subjected to business school training" (p. 9). The critics argue that business school faculty members teach such concepts as transaction-based economics, economic liberalism, or agency theory to students, which focus on short-term profits even if this comes at a cost of damaging long-term opportunities and relationships with customers, suppliers, and/or vendors (Mitroff, 2004, p. 185). Ghoshal states that "business schools have actively freed their students from any sense of moral responsibility" because faculty members teach theories that are ideological in nature (2005, p. 76). The business school faculty members provide training and consult with retailers in variety of businesses in the service industry. Similarly, business students end up working with and managing businesses in the service industry. A report from the *Wall Street Journal* (February 6th of 1996) stated that 44% of restaurant and fast-food services employees said they steal cash or merchandise. This report also states, that employees who "filch the occasional note pad, pen or light bulb" costs American businesses about $120 billion each year; this study had been conducted by Jerald Greenberg, professor of business ethics at Ohio State University. It seems as though more top level executives are committing fraud (Schroeder, 1996) and illegal acts such as insider trading, doctors are being caught operating under the influence of drugs, and others are being found to be practicing without licenses (Wood, 1990). Everybody is talking about ethics and morality, but nobody seems surprised by the decrease in lack of ethics and moral behavior (Wood, 1990).

Solomon (1994) states that unethical thinking isn't just bad business; it is an invitation to disaster in business. Rarely, however, is unethical behavior actually found out and punished. According to Solomon, a survey (completed on Sept. 1991) found that 63 percent of the participants say they do not enjoy their work and about half blame a "dog-eat-dog" climate in their firms--less than 10 percent complained about low pay.

Nash (1994) states that business people have recognized the high cost of unethical behavior and its causes. Corporate scandals have created heavy fines, disruption of normal routine, low employee morale, internal fraud, and loss of public confidence in the reputation of a company. Nash further states that business leaders emphasize that high personal standard of conduct are a major asset to a company. Executives' high personal standard can create an environment where people are happy and motivated to accomplish organizational objectives because they feel proud to work there.

Today's marketplace demands a more sophisticated approach in ethical dilemmas; one that is more than simply game-playing or acting-out based on personal feelings. Nash (1994) states that integrity in today's business requires a strong holding power, so it can hold together a multitude of different conflicting values and encourage personal morality and management concerns in the same dimension.

Public awareness of business ethics and unethical behaviors have increased in the past decade (DeGeorge 1995, Sims 1994). DeGeorge and Sims, both mention that business ethics has gone through some developmental periods.

First, there was the period before the 1960's where people discussed ethics in business for example issues regarding just wages, decent conditions of employment, and honesty in business dealings. In the 1960's the United States saw the rise of social issues in business. These were the years of the Vietnam War, the emergence of counterculture, the awareness of environmental issues, and the rise of consumer movements. The 1970's saw the rise of business ethics. The term business ethics was modeled after the medical ethics term, which had been adopted by those interested in medical ethics. This period brought about corporate internationalization and new markets in Asia and the Middle-East which shifted the corporate conscience to the issue of bribery here and abroad (Nash, 1994). In 1976, the American Assembly of Collegiate Schools of Business (AACSB) urged business educators to integrate ethics into their curricula (Bishop, 1992). The period of the 1980's could be called the movement of business ethics era. A number of Fortune Five Hundred companies had adopted corporate ethical codes, where ethical committees and task forces were formed. Some companies even had ethics "hotlines", where employees could register their ethical concerns (Nash, 1994).

By the 1990's, the government also had become involved in business ethics. A number of judges mandated corporate-wide ethics training in some companies that had been found guilty of fraud or other illegal acts. In 1991, Congress enacted Federal Sentencing Guidelines which could apply to corporations that were found guilty of breaking laws. In 1994, the House of Representatives also passed the Congressional Ethics Reform Act to prevent members of the Congress and their staff from accepting gifts or even lunches from their constituents. Sims (1994) states that if unethical actions continue as they did in 1992 and 1993 in organizations, then a new era of public concern, consciousness, and legislation could be seen in the near future. This will be caused by businesses' inability to prevent immoral behaviors and protect the consumers. It is clear that the 1990's has brought business ethics into an interdisciplinary field of study, with the development of various research activities which help to define this new and emerging field.

Definition of Business Ethics

Nash (1994) states that ethics is the study of how one's personal moral norms apply to the goals and activities of businesses. She states that business ethics is not a separate moral standard, but the study of how the business context poses its own unique problems for the moral person who acts on the behalf of the business. She states that business ethics generally falls into one of the three areas of management decision-making. First, the choices about the laws, that is, what should the law be and whether or not to obey it. Second, choices about the economic and social issues which are beyond the law's domain, which are also called peoples' values. Thirdly, choices about the pre-eminence of one's own self-interest, that is, whether it should come before the company or other people involved.

According to DeGeorge (1995), business ethics as a field is defined by the interaction of ethics and business. He also states that business ethics is as national and international, as business itself, and there are no geographical boundaries that could limit it. There are five kinds of activities in business ethics (DeGeorge, 1995). The first is the application of general ethical principles to a particular case or practice in business. The second one should investigate whether moral terms which are used to describe individuals and the actions they perform can be applied to other enterprises as well. The third activity of business ethics is the analysis of the moral presuppositions of business, and from a moral point of view. One must question the morality of economic systems in general. The fourth activity of business is to solve ethical problems from a different philosophical perspective. This would require one to enter another domain of knowledge, such as economic or organizational theory. The fifth activity of business ethics is to create moral ideals for people in organizations so everyone can look up to them and follow their examples.

According to Cooke (1986), business ethics should be a systematic attempt to integrate models of ethical behavior with the day-to-day moral problems of the business world. Some examples of this would be the court rulings based on improper or unethical decisions of business leaders in organizations. Phillips (1995) states that corporations are generally liable for the unethical acts within the scope of their employment, committed by directors, managers, and employees. Phillips also reports that in the case of United States vs. Bank of New England; in 1987, the trial court had issued a jury charge stating that:

> You have to look at the bank as an institution. As such, its knowledge is the sum of the knowledge of all of the employees. That is, the bank's knowledge is the totality of what all of the employees know with the scope of their employment. So, if employee A knows one facet of the currency reporting requirement, B knows another facet of it, and C knows a third facet of it, then the bank knows them all. (p. 562)

In such a case, corporations are liable for their decisions which cause harm to others. Walton (1990) mentions a case of 1742, the Charitable Corporation vs. Sir Robert Sulton, where directors of the company were held responsible for failing to monitor the behavior of managers whose embezzlements and fraudulent receipts led to the company's bankruptcy. He further states that for years the focus was on the 1985 case of Smith vs. Gorkum, in which the Delaware Supreme Court stated that the directors of the company failed to use the relevant information available to recommend a cash-buy-out merger proposal. So, the directors had breached their fiduciary responsibilities to the shareholders. Phillips (1995) concludes that just as we are less apt to excuse adults for submitting to delusions rather than we are children, we also should try to expect higher standards from corporations than we expect from its members. This is because corporations have greater capacity than their individual components, and thus they should be held to higher standards.

Are there Ethics in Business?

DeGeorge (1995) states that ethics always has been in business and the subject of business ethics is neither new nor any different from ethics in other areas. Drucker (1994) mentions that ethics is not a recent discovery; however, business ethics rapidly is becoming the "in" subject, replacing yesterdays "social responsibility." He further states that to the moralist of the Western tradition, "business ethics" would make no sense at all, since the moralist of Western tradition do not agree with "business ethics." All authorities in the Western tradition agree there is only one ethics, one set of rules of morality, that of individual behavior in which the same rules apply to everyone alike. Drucker (1994) uses the example of

Lockheed paying bribes to the Japanese who considered buying planes and compares it to the pedestrian in New York's Central Park handing his wallet over to a mugger. Everyone condemned Lockheed's act as immoral; however, no one would consider the pedestrian to have acted immorally. Here, it does not seem fair that business ethics views corporations to have acted immorally in cases of extortion while human beings are treated as victims.

Contrary to Drucker's ideas, Collins (1994) suggests that business ethics may not make sense to the traditional managers; however, the current view of management holds ethics as an essential part of doing business. There are many people who think that it is impossible to be an effective business manager and a moral individual simultaneously. Collins states that management effectiveness and individual ethics are not mutually exclusive, which is why there are many people desiring to be managers. He further concludes that business and ethics are not contradictory and that good ethics is synonymous with good management. Traditionally, it has been viewed that profit maximization is the exclusive goal of managers; and ethics is viewed as having consideration for others. So, there is a concern for one-self and a concern for others which makes these views clash. Collins (1994) states that business managers could rely on the utilitarian view of ethics and the deontologist's view of ethics. The utilitarian argues that actions are moral if they produce the greatest benefit to the largest number of people. The deontologist believes that in order to determine whether an action is moral, then one must have valid ethical principles to apply to the problem. Deontologists claim that individuals have rights and are entitled to justice, as opposed to the social utility principle of the utilitarians.

Collins (1994) combines the traditional principles of the utilitarian and deontologist to create a new principle; that is, to create value for all stakeholders of the organization and build trust amongst all stakeholders. This view has a more practical value for managers than the traditional views (Cavanagh, Moberg & Velasquez, 1995). It is the responsibility of management, therefore to create value by expanding the concept of customers to include all stakeholders. It is also the responsibility of the managers to build trust by respecting and honoring each individual's autonomy and provide them with help as they need it.

It is the deontological theory of justice, rights, and fairness that explains why insider trading is immoral and illegal (Cavinagh, Moberg & Velasquez, 1995). Shefrin and Statman (1993) state that those who view management as profit-seekers seem to over-look that the regulation of financial markets is shaped by considerations that go beyond efficiency or self-interest. These considerations include concerns for ethical issues and fairness (Shefrin & Statman, 1993).

By law, insider trading is illegal, and most individuals and corporations believe it to be immoral. The most important reason insider trading is illegal is because it undermines the fiduciary relationship that lies at the heart of American business (Moore, 1990). Some people think insider trading is unfair because everyone does not have "equal" information or "equal access" to information. This argument is not very clear because most people will choose a field in order to gain knowledge and access to information which others are not capable of learning quickly. Attorneys justify their fees because they have knowledge which others are lacking. An insider trader can argue that he or she chose this profession to acquire such knowledge and to use it to his or her benefit. Moore (1990) argues that insider trading is not wrong because of fairness, but because a breach of fiduciary duty is involved.

It would be very difficult and costly for corporations to prohibit and monitor inside trading. However, it is the responsibility of the firm to prohibit the use of its property, that is, inside information, because it is morally wrong. If insider information is really the property of the firm that produces it, then using that property is wrong only when the firm prohibits it (Moore, 1990). Companies have an obligation to the community and society in general to address such issues and to practice ethics to their fullest extent throughout the organization.

Wolfe (1993) states that business ethics is not a course to be taught; rather, it is a moral system that needs to be examined throughout the entire educational process. He further states that business ethics courses are a "drop in the river" of heavy mental conditioning for capitalism. He states that courses in business ethics should be called "The Study of Corporate and Professional Social Responsibility," because students learn how to become socially responsible in the business environment. In the United States there are about 600,000 undergraduate business ethics students graduating every year, and about 100,000 students at the graduate level. Wolfe (1993) further states that students should learn the moral law of capitalism, which states that business life is competition, that is "lions eat lambs" and the strong are preferred, and they deserve all they can own and control.

Corporate Moral and Social Responsibility

Ostapski and Isaacs (1992) state that moral responsibility should be a self-imposed obligation to ensure that actions and decisions of human beings do not cause harm to others. Moral responsibility usually is both ascribed and assumed by individuals who participate in the making of the corporation or its decisions (Phillips, 1995). These decisions affect other stakeholders of the company, including the society and the environment in general. The consequences of such a decision could decrease or increase the interest of stakeholders in the company. This is why the decisions of each individual, from upper management to lower management, is extremely important to corporate and social responsibility (Phillips, 1995).

Hoffman (1994) suggests that corporations should develop and act out of a moral corporate culture in order for them to be seen as a morally responsible company. He states that America's excellent companies have a clear understanding of what they stand for, and are serious about the process of value which shapes their corporate culture from a moral point of view. Hoffman further states that corporations must regulate themselves morally because society expects it and morality demands it. Also, it is true that there is a connection between business excellence and morally sensitive corporate culture (Hoffman, 1994).

Organizational culture is commonly defined as the way things are done in each business, and the question of how they are done takes precedence over why they are done. So, in order to change a culture, then it is essential to talk about ethics (Drummond & Bain, 1994). Ethics is the only effective change mechanism in corporate culture because it asks why things are done. Drummond and Bain further state that changing a corporate culture without ethics is like changing a tire without a jack, because cultures can be very strong and they are very difficult to change.

Research has shown that corporate and individual ethical decision-making leads to less fear and less hostility. According to a report in the *Wall Street Journal* (April 11, 1991), a survey of 111 executives concluded, "The more `emotionally healthy' the executives, as measured on a battery of test, the more likely they were to score high on the ethics test. Executives who scored high were also less likely to feel hostility, anxiety and fear" (Solomon, 1994). John Kotter and James Haskett (1992) studied the link between strong ethical cultures in a company and economic performance. They found that those companies which took seriously their responsibilities to their employees and customers had four times as much revenues as those who did not. Companies not only produced revenue on average of about four times more, but their profits and stocks rose about 750 percent and 900 percent respectively.

Each corporation is made up of individuals, from different backgrounds and cultures, who think and act as moral agents for the corporation. So, a responsible corporation also should allow for the moral autonomy of each individual within its culture (Hoffman, 1994), because it is the individuals who can carry out all their responsibilities smoothly, effectively, and timely.

Solomon (1994) suggests that social responsibility of corporations depends on the nature of the corporation and what it is capable of doing. Corporations should be responsible to what the society is demanding of it (Rogers, 1994). Some companies may help in their communities by sponsoring athletics programs for teenagers and those who are mentally challenged, and others might help in cleaning the environment in the community.

Corporations are not moral agents and they are not morally responsible for corporate actions (Velasquez, 1988; Ostapski & Isaacs, 1992) because they are established by rational human beings to achieve specific objectives. It is the individuals in the corporation who have been given the authority to make decisions for the corporation, so they also should be accountable for these decisions as well. Velasquez argues that individuals should not be sacrificed for the good of the corporations by instructing them not to think but just act according to policy, instead they should be given accountability and responsibility for their actions.

Friedman (1994) believes that the purpose of business is to maximize profit, and executives are hired by owners to act as agents in the interest of the shareholders. He believes that business people should not exercise social responsibility in their capacity as company executives, because social responsibility does not increase shareholders' wealth. He further states that exercising social responsibility costs money because the company must invest in the work-hours needed to contemplate on the consequences of its socially responsible actions.

Albert Carr (1994) seems to have taken Friedman's positions, to some extent, when it comes to social responsibility. Carr states that ethics in business is not similar to ethics in general, but rather is similar to the ethics of a poker game. In his view, if one intends to be a winner in the business environment, then he/she should have a "game player's" attitude. Business decisions should be impersonal and geared toward company objectives. If a supermarket manager, for example, orders the rotten tomatoes to be discarded, he/she does this to avoid customer complaints and the loss of good will. Carr concludes:

So long as a business person complies with the law of the land and avoids telling malicious lies, he's ethical. If the law as written gives a man a wide-open chance to make a killing, he would be a fool not to take advantage of it. If he doesn't, someone else will. If the law says he can do it, then that is all the justification he needs. (p. 31)

Carr states that business people seek money and power, which they will try to obtain without breaking the law. He further states that all sensible business people prefer to tell the truth; however, they seldom feel inclined to tell the whole truth. In the majority of cases, according to Carr, business people tell the truth to avoid possible problems and to "save face." He concludes that companies should obey laws and should shape their strategies without reference to social responsibility, only profits.

According to DeGeorge (1995) and Phillips (1995), each corporation is morally responsible for its actions and decisions to the public and the society in general, because corporations have a mandate to do business for society's benefit. They are morally obligated not to harm anyone as a result of their actions. DeGeorge believes that corporations are legal entities, so they are obligated by law to act legally. People within a corporation make decisions on behalf of it, so if an act is unethical for the person, then it should be unethical for the organization as well (Phillips, 1995). DeGeorge (1995) states that all ethical decisions should consider the long-term effects of each action as it relates to all stakeholders.

Gellerman (1986) states that ambitious managers often try to outperform their peers by increasing the short-term benefits of their decisions and ignoring the long-term effects. In our society, rewards generally are based on short-term performance (Nagy & Obenberger, 1994), which further reinforces the short-term results. Gellerman (1986), Ostapski and Issace (1992) discuss several companies that went out of business because their leaders did not make ethical decisions, for example, Manville Corporation and Continental Illinois Bank. They also mention how corporate leaders can make socially responsible decisions that affect their future and the society in general. An example of this would be Johnson and Johnson's decision to recall its Tylenol products, which many consider as a socially responsible action. According to Preston Jones (1993), this took serious discussion and "brainstorming" sessions between top level executives of Johnson and Johnson. The decision had to be made quickly and responsibly, which is why the company recaptured the majority of its market share and enhanced its public image simultaneously. Its decision was made easier because of their Corporate Credo which stresses service for the public good (Ostapski & Isaacs, 1992). It has been suggested that corporate social responsibility should be self-imposed by a strong commitment in order to eliminate all harm caused by the corporation. Since not all legal actions are moral, corporate decision should go beyond the letter of the law in order for the corporation to be considered as a morally responsible corporation.

Organizational Climate and Ethical Behavior

There has been much research done in the area of organizational climate and its relationship to ethical behavior and managerial influence over associates (Badenhorst, 1994). Some of the researchers have studied organizational climate in the context of warmth and support (Field & Abelson, 1982), nature of rewards (Schneider & Reichers, 1983), absenteeism (Victor & Cullen, 1987), and achievement (Litwin & Stringer, 1968). The thrust of the above research is that business ethics is good for business (Carmichael & Drummond, 1989; Donaldson & Davis, 1990), and essential for the survival of the business (Phillips, 1995; DeGeorge, 1995).

Buamhart (1961) surveyed executives and concluded that, if an executive acts ethically, this is attributable to his own set of values and his ability to resist pressure and temptation, with credit due to his superiors for being good examples and company policy as well. He also stated that, if an executive commits an immoral act, it is largely because of his superiors and the climate of industry ethics. Badenhorst (1994) concluded that the causes of unethical behavior are not necessarily the individual's lack of standards. The unethical act could be caused by many variables such as pressure from others (Brenner, 1992) or cultural differences. Past research has also suggested that actions of managers, the ethical climate of the firm, and the absence of a company policy on moral issues are all contributing factors which produce unethical behavior (Badenhorst, 1995).

Past research also has concluded that organizational climate is a very important factor in shaping the behavior of employees (Schneider, 1975; Badenhorst, 1994; Brenner, 1992). Fleishmans' (1953) and Brenners' (1992) research studies have concluded that foremen adapt their behavior to the prevailing climate in a factory by behaving, not as they were taught in school or other human relations programs, but in a style consistent with their work environment. Most of the research cases in the area of organizational climate consistently have proven that people will change their ethical behavior to match the environment's climate. Another study done by Litwin and Stringer (1968), found that people will adapt their leadership behavior to the organizational climate and the leaders' ethical standards. There is evidence which states that there is a significant relationship between organizational climate, peoples' behavior (Dieterly & Schneider, 1974) and peer pressures (Stephenson, Galbraith & Grimm, 1995).

Like any other type of organizational climate, it should be expected that ethical climate is linked to a range of behaviors as well (Wimbush & Shepard, 1994). In this case, ethical behaviors and possibly even counterproductive behaviors, such as absenteeism and turnover, may all be linked to organizational performance. Ethical climate has been defined as stable, psychologically meaningful, and shared perceptions that employees hold concerning ethical procedures and policies which may exist in their organizations (Schneider, 1975).

The expression "a picture is a thousand words" implies that people learn better by example of real-life occurrences (Schaupp & Lane, 1992) than lectures and reading of policies. This also reinforces the saying "seeing is believing," because actions speak louder than words and people will behave as they see their leaders in action. The human mind has been trained to see and think in pictures as our thought processes continue to function (Trudeau, 1992). Sometimes these pictures can be so vivid, clear, and descriptive that the mind will not be able to tell the difference between reality and imagination (Trudeau, 1992). Since the mind cannot always differentiate between reality and imagination, then we can say that human mind is very powerful and it can pressure us to act immorally, if it has a joyful picture of the end result.

If the organization is encouraging the "bottom line" as profit, then everyone can foresee getting rewarded if they achieve higher profits, especially in the short term (Maremont, 1995). It is the reward which the mind is picturing and it can have a great amount of influence on the individual decision-making process (Trudeaw, 1992). Corporate managers need to think of the consequences of each issue while making such decisions as rewarding individuals based on higher sales and in making such decisions, ethical behavior should take precedence over the bottom line (Solomon, 1994). Increased sales are consequences of satisfied customers, so it makes sense to reward people based on increased and satisfied customers instead of higher sales for a short period of time. Therefore, organizations need to have built-in ethics systems in their decision-making process (Gellerman, 1986). This means emphasizing and rewarding ethical behavior in all situations.

In the traditional methods we have always viewed ethical behavior based on the Golden Rule, "do unto others as you would have them do unto you." There is one giant assumption which the golden rule holds that prevents the application of this rule in the present society. The assumption is that everyone's values in our societies are the same and currently this is not the case in most nations (Hosmer, 1994). Moral standards of behavior differ between people because their goals, norms, beliefs, and values upon which they are based on are different.

The awareness of corruptions and violations of ethical behavior seem to imply that ethics in America is getting more attention and more awareness (Woods, 1990). This attention and awareness can mean that we are noticing and caring about ethical issues, and that we are expecting everyone to act and behave morally. This awareness could be forcing "Corporate America" to take a second look at the moral values and standards which they present (Phillips, 1995). This could be the era which pushes corporations to have more objectives that will enhance their ethical behavior, and it also could help top executives realize that "bottom line" should not be considered to be the only purpose of business (Nagy, 1994; DeGeorge, 1995).

Demographic Influences on Moral Behavior

The majority of researchers have studied two demographic variables which are more likely to be related to moral judgments; and those variables are gender and age differences. There is an increased participation of women in the workplace today, and they are entering more top level positions than ever before (Dawson, 1995). It has been shown that some moral development theorists believe that men and women vary in their ethical decision-making. Dawson surveyed 48 males and 40 females who were between the ages of 26 to 62, and had about 2 to 36 years of experience. Dawson's results support Gilligan's theory that men and women bring different ethical standards and values to the workforce. Women seem to be compassionate, and men appear more objective. Women show concern for relationships and feelings, while males are more concerned with rights and rules. Sikula and Costa (1994) surveyed male and female college students and concluded that men and women college students are ethically equivalent. Their results also found that men and women significantly vary in four non-ethical values. They stated that, compared to men, women value a world at peace and the notion of forgiving more, and an exciting life and being imaginative less.

Ford and Richarson (1994) found that about half of the literature pertaining to gender differences found that at least in some situations females are more ethical than men; however, the other half of the results found no difference based on gender. The studies also show that each sex rates the other more unethical than themselves (Kidwell et al., 1987). Age also can account in moral decision making of individuals, because people gain more experience and develop a more sophisticated view of the world as they grow older (Piaget, 1975; Kohlberg, 1984; Gilligan, 1982). There seems to be a clear consensus between researcher findings that older managers are more ethical than younger managers (Carroll, 1975); and younger managers feel as though they are under pressure to compromise their ethical standards (Posner & Schmidt, 1987; Baumhart, 1961). They also conclude that managers under 40 years of age thought their ethical standards did not match their organizations. It also has been shown that managers employed for a long period of time were more moral in their responses than managers who had worked just a few years.

Since the influence of superiors and peers has a great impact on ones behavior, researchers believe that younger people and those who are new to their jobs are more affected by this influence than older people and those who have been in the company for a longer period of time (Arlow & Ulrich, 1988). It may not be certain whether men are more ethical than women or visa-versa; however it is certain that more females are coming into the workforce and are bringing about differences as to how ethical problems are perceived and solved in the business environment. Organizational training programs should consider the content of the program from both perspectives of males and females, because they each have their advantages. Both genders seem to have the ability to develop better ethical judgment as they gain experience and grow older (Gilligan, 1982).

Influences of Managers on Ethical Behavior

Wimbush and Shepard (1994) state that supervisors' decisions can have a great impact on organizational climate and behavior. Fortunately, more of the supervisors and top level managers are able to recognize ethical situations, due to corporate codes of ethics and ethics training. In 1983, the *Wall Street Journal* published the results of a survey conducted by the Gallup Organization. They surveyed 1,558 adults from a national sample and 396 mid-level corporate managers to discover the consistency of ethical beliefs amongst the public and corporate managers. While 49 percent of the public felt that the business ethical standards had declined, only 23 percent of the corporate managers believed this and about 33 percent of the managers felt that business ethical standards had risen. More of today's top level management are trying to consider their decisions from an ethical point of view. They either have a code of ethics or they have a strong commitment for moral behavior throughout their companies. Proper corporate ethical emphasis and training affect the behavior and attitude of managers, which in turn could have a major impact on their employees (Murphy, Smith & Daley, 1992).

Managers at different levels based on their age and experience could view moral dilemmas differently. Carroll's (1975) survey concluded that young managers as well as lower and middle level managers, felt pressure from their superiors to compromise their ethical values in order to achieve results. Managers have been pressured by their superiors to meet target sales (Maremont, 1995), and to change sales and profit numbers in order to receive benefits (Wallace, 1995). Western (1995) states that today it is difficult to keep secrets, and thus the best solution is to "run faster" than the competitors and educate employees about company standards, values and moral issues.

Using role-playing to integrate ethics in business curriculum will help students get more practical experience while dealing with ethical issues (Brown, 1994). One could conclude that corporate emphasis on moral behavior does make a difference on how its managers and employees see an ethical situation. Researchers have suggested that corporations should try to emphasize ethical behavior; otherwise, it may cost the company its reputation and its survival (Gellerman, 1986).

Some business leaders think ethics will take care of itself; and this type of thinking may result in unethical acts that harm innocent people in the society (DeGeorge, 1995). This is why the government is interfering with private industry by regulating most of its decision making. Most businesses suffer from the regulations because few businesses have failed to act morally or in good faith. Businesses should be concerned with ethics (DeGeorge, 1995) because, eventually, it affects their bottom line (Solomon, 1994) in one way or the other, and most likely adversely if they have no ethical strategy.

Freedom does not mean we are allowed to do anything and everything. The free market depends on following the rules of fair play and respecting people as well as their belongings. Regulations are needed for businesses and should exist to a certain extent in order to protect the interest of the consumers (Carr, 1994). Yet, we cannot make a rule about every single issue because that would just be too costly, possibly causing a disaster, and thus it would discourage entrepreneurship (Takala & Uusitalo, 1995). There are 41,000 regulations in America for the production, distribution and selling of hamburgers (Solomon, 1994). For example, in 1993, there were over 10,000 injuries caused by First Aid Kits, and there are over 4,000 pen related accidents every year in America (Solomon, 1994). Most of these accidents were never meant to happen, but they are accidents caused by carelessness and unfortunate circumstances which no regulation can stop from happening. For example, in 1994 a 19 year old student at the University of Florida, this author's brother, observed his calculus professor lecturing about the importance of math. The professor threw his pen on the floor and jumped on it up and down about five or six times and yelled "this is how we treat math in America and as a nation we are behind in our math scores." This act obviously left a lasting impression on this student, because during the next week when his sister asked him to help her with a high school calculus problem, he repeated his professor's act and threw his pencil on the carpet and stepped on it up and down, without having shoes on, about two or three times, before the sharp end of the pencil went through the bottom of his foot and came out from the top while bleeding profusely. This explains that this was an accident waiting to happen, and regulation may not be able to stop this from happening (Takala & Uusitalo, 1995). This incident also suggests that we learn to adapt the behavior of our mentors, role models, parents, teachers, and our superiors at work. So, teaching and practicing moral behaviors will always benefit those who are watching and learning either in the class or at work stations.

When it comes to ethics, the expression "walking your talk" serves as the foundation of ethical behavior; and thus, the ethical conduct of mentors and role models are extremely important. As prior research has shown, ethical behavior of individual managers and top executives plays a major role in shaping their employees' ethical standards (Wimbush & Shepard, 1994). Freeman and Gilbert (1988) concluded that if corporate strategy does not recognize the internal and external values and goals of its members, then those members could not be expected to achieve organizational goals. It is extremely important that ethical values of a company are observed, agreed upon and understood by members in order to institutionalize morality and other codes of conduct (Sims, 1994).

Cross-Cultural Studies of Ethics
The basic variable of ethical behavior on the international level has been similar to national research but with more emphasis on nationality representing the cultural behavior of individuals and the norms with which they had to comply (Ford & Richardson, 1994). The majority of international researchers examine nationality, religion, sex, age, education, employment, and personality variables to determine the moral behavior of individuals. Kohlberg (1984) states that no significant differences have been found in moral development of individuals due to their religious beliefs.

There are mixed results on some variables as they relate to different cultures and nationalities. Izraeli (1988), as well as Tsalkis and Nwachakwu (1988, 1989), concluded that culture has little or no impact on ethical beliefs. Abratt, Nel, and Higgs (1992) found no difference in the ethical responses of managers from South Africa and Australia. They concluded, therefore, that despite the existence of different socio-cultural and political factors, managers' ethical beliefs are similar; and culture has little or no impact on ethical belief, thus supporting previous findings. They also mention that honesty, integrity, self-discipline, and loyalty are part of every civilization; however, the levels of adherence and commitment varies among people. While the Hegarty and Sims (1978, 1979), as well as the White and Rhodeback (1992) studies, showed significant correlations between unethical behavior and non-U.S. citizenship; Becker and Fritzche (1987) studied the degree to which French, German, and U.S. managers differed in believing that codes of conduct were effective in influencing managerial behavior, with the French having the greatest faith in these ethical codes or devices.

A study completed by Tope Adeyemi-Bello from East Carolina University (1994) indicated that Nigerian males and females in general have similar work values (Adeyemi-Bello, 1994). In another study, Honeycutt, Sibuaw, and Hunt (1995) found that customer orientation in U.S. and Taiwan was influenced by ethics training. They also suggested that managers should evaluate current ethics training programs to insure that correct ethical behavior is taught and rewarded. This is important because most people will perform based on the expected rewards. Maremont (1995) reports that Ray-Bans' Hong Kong unit reported fake sales in recent years in order to meet sales targets. Rewards that are based on sales could cause people to act unethically, and should be considered very carefully (Honeycutt, Siguaw & Hunt, 1995).

Moral values are part of one's culture (Morris, 1982). Hindu children learn to value life in all of its forms, while most Americans generally learn that only human life is important – even then, some American military leaders tend to say collateral damage is unavoidable (and perhaps acceptable) in some cases when fighting insurgents as has been demonstrated in the unfortunate conflicts in the occupation of Iraq over the past five years. DeGeorge (1995) states that justice is in part determined by the system in which a particular practice is evaluated, which could include its constitution, laws, commonly accepted customs, values, beliefs, and other social norms. By this, he means that two cultures can see the same issue in two different ways; yet they both can be morally right because they can defend their practice by their own point of view.

In some cases, people can have different points of view about an issue within the same culture. For example, some people believe in abortion and some do not. Each side can provide its own moral justification for the issue. At one time, slavery was not judged as immoral; however, times have changed; and people of the same culture can have different views in different times because situations vary and more variables can come into the light. As DeGeorge states, liberal theory tends toward the position that there is no one single system of values, beliefs, and practices. DeGeorge (1995) concludes that different systems can be just and justice does not require that all nations adopt the same view of justice.

Ethical behavior of people can vary from country to country because it is subject to the influence of regulatory environment and cultural framework (Lee, Tse, Vertinsky & Wehrung, 1994). Lee et al. (1994) completed a study on comparison of manager's perceptions in the People's Republic of China, Hong Kong, and Canada. They suggest that responsible business behavior can be different in each country because of the regulatory differences and rewards (Honeycutt et al., 1995) which exist in each country. For example, in the People's Republic of China, firms can afford to invest into huge projects without being concerned about going bankrupt, because they are part of the state-enterprise, so there is no possibility of bankruptcy. In Hong Kong, however, all the rewards and responsibilities are distributed to individuals in charge of the enterprises. The culture forces people to do a good job, and those who do a good job get the respect of everyone in the community. People will go out of their way to make responsible decisions for the corporation. Managers in Canada seem to be somewhat in the middle of the two preceding situations. It is clear who is responsible for the success of the firm, and each person takes accountability for his or her decisions without losing respect. Managers in the People's Republic of China were found to favor a "win-win" situation for all firms involved in the transaction. While managers in Hong Kong and Canada were less likely to be concerned about the "win-win" situation. Their data, thus, showed that regulatory environment and collective cultures can have a significant impact on a manager's business decisions. These can be viewed moral in one country while totally immoral in view of a different culture with different regulations.

Honeycutt, Siguaw, and Hunt (1995) completed a cross-cultural study of managers in United States and Taiwan. They found ethics training to be negatively related to perceived levels of morality and performance. Salespeople with high performance records reported high ethical behavior, while the opposite was found to be true in Taiwan. They also found that ethics training did influence the customer orientation of managers in both countries. They suggested developing a strong ethics training program for those companies that are seeking greater customer orientation to remain competitive.

Institutionalizing Ethics

Bishop (1992) points out a criticism of ethics which states that as long as there are laws that dictate what is permissible, there is no need to teach ethics in classes. Many agree that it is important to act with the intent of the law, instead of following the letter of the law, because there are many loopholes which can exist in written laws. Bishop also points out that we should try to differentiate between acting legally and acting ethically. Sims (1994) states that some companies like Salomon Brother and E. F. Hutton assumed that the ethical side of business would take care of itself, and some other companies like Heinz also assumed that a signed statement from senior executives would take care of immoral behavior. Each assumption proved to be wrong.

People define "ethical" business differently; however, if a company sets business standards based on its core values, then employees can be expected to play by the rules (Richter & Barnum, 1994). These standards should be written and communicated on daily basis. The Center for Business Ethics at Bentley College, in Waltham, Mass., found in 1991, that 45 percent of the 1,000 largest U.S. companies have some type of ethics programs or workshops, and this figure is up from 35 percent five years earlier (Solomon, 1994). It has been demonstrated that instruction in business' moral obligation can cause present and future managers to internalize more responsible values which will help them to be more ethical (Phillips, 1995). Honeycutt et al. (1995) found that ethics training helped managers to be more customer oriented. Many corporations and schools are teaching special classes in social responsibility and ethics. The content of these classes vary from ethical awareness, where increasing sensitivity to moral dilemmas at work are discussed, to ethical reasoning which discusses different learning strategies for solving moral dilemmas. Bishop (1992) states that education serves to reinforce existing values and encourage their application. Art Wolfe (1993) states that business ethics is a moral system which should be examined and integrated throughout the entire educational or learning process.

Sims (1994) reports that approximately 80 percent of the largest corporations have a formal ethics program and about 44 percent provide ethics training, supporting previous studies. Critics argue that ethics cannot be taught because it is based on values, and values are learned at an early age before one starts to work. They also claim that ethics cannot be learned in a formal way; instead, it is learned by example.

The supporters of ethics training programs claim that values can be learned and changed, even after the childhood stages (Shaw & Barry, 1992). This has been proven by Kohlberg's (1984) stages of moral development, which indicates that learning does not stop in adolescence but can continue until the mid-thirties. Like culture, ethical and unethical behaviors are learned and developed in response to each situation. Sims (1994) suggested that ethical behaviors can be learned and unethical behaviors can be unlearned. The most important reason for ethics training is to increase awareness of ethical dilemmas in the work environment (Honeycutt et al., 1995).

It has been suggested that ethical awareness programs should start at the orientation programs of each new associate (Sims, 1994). Emphasis should come from the top down, and it should be a continuous process of reinforcement. Sims (1994) suggests that the discussion should be relevant to the work environment, and should be geared toward immediate and personal issues which associates are likely to encounter every day. Also, employee participation should be included as much as possible to make the learning process more interesting and to encourage cognitive development.

It is extremely essential that top management reflects and reinforces ethical behavior (Shaw & Barry, 1992). This can be done by training, which is an important vehicle to institutionalize ethics and to encourage ethical behavior. Also, the entire organization must agree on the importance of ethical values and there must be a standardized procedure that everyone in the organization can follow. Ethics, therefore, can be learned just like any other subject, and if it does not help change unethical behavior, then at least it creates an awareness that certain acts will not be tolerated in the organization.

American firms are more involved in ethics training and ethics programs than other nations (Solomon, 1994). This is due to the increased competition between corporations and the fact that they are all trying to earn consumers' trust. Corporations are trying to increase the wealth and value of their primary and secondary stakeholder groups. Top executives are realizing that without the support of primary stakeholders (customers, employees, suppliers, government, etc.) they will not be able to continue successfully (Clarkson, 1995). Clarkson also states that, without the support of the secondary stakeholders (media, political parties, etc.), the primary stakeholders may not continue their support.

The fundamental question of ethics is "good individuals exist, how are they possible?" The answer to this question is that good people exist because they can afford to, they are compelled to, and because they are inspired to (Nicholson, 1994). Firstly, this tells us that moral decision-making should be geared toward doing the right thing each time. Secondly, people should be obligated to act morally because they believe it is the right thing to do, and because it is part of their organizational credo. Thirdly, moral behavior should get inspired by the company in a public way. This will build commitment and strengthen moral values in all individuals. This training and reinforcement process should come from the top and it should be in all phases of the company.

Leaders can institutionalize the process of ethical decision-making by ensuring that each moral decision builds upon the decisions that proceed it (Stoner & Freeman, 1989). Institutionalizing ethical policies can be done by training, corporate codes of ethics, ethics committees, and other ethics seminars or orientation programs, as well as a combination of the above programs.

Corporate Codes of Conduct

Corporate ethics programs are part of organizational life and they exist whether management purposely creates them or not (Brenner, 1992). Most of these programs are not created purposely, but are inherent in the cultural environment of the processes of the firm. It has been found in a recent study that pressures within informal systems can be a dominant influence in the resolution of ethical issues (Falkenberg & Herremans, 1995). Corporate codes of ethics should protect individuals and should address the moral values of individuals in their decision-making processes (Badenhorst, 1994). Corporate codes of ethics are not merely some manuals for how-to-solve problems. They are tools which can empower everyone in the organization to say, "I am sorry that is against our policy or that would violate our company's code of ethics" (Hosmer, 1994). This will make the decision-making process much easier; it will save time and costs which might be associated with other decisions (Solomon, 1994). This also will increase personal commitment of employees to their companies because people do take pride in the integrity of their corporate culture (Dean, 1992). Dean states that businesses must provide a comprehensive code of ethics, as well as training (Badenhorst, 1994), for every high level manager to think, speak, and to act ethically. A written code of conduct is the first and most effective measure which can be taken against unethical behavior (Badenhorst, 1994). This code of ethics should specifically spell out policies and guidelines for the day-to-day operation of the company.

Drucker (1994) states that an effective organizational code of ethics, one that deserves to be seriously considered as "ethics," will have to define "right" behavior as conduct which maximizes each party's benefits, and thus makes the relationship harmonious, constructive, and mutually beneficial.

Hosmer (1994) defined ethical codes as statements which describe the norms and beliefs of an organization, which is the way individual members should think. Hosmer also defined ethical rules as requirements to act in a certain way, which is what each individual must do in given situations.

A Conference Board Survey which included 264 corporations from the United States, Europe, Mexico, and Canada showed the following results (Solomon, 1994): first, some 84 percent of U.S. firms that responded had an ethics code, and the figure for non-American firms were 58 percent; second, only 57 percent of financial firms had ethics codes, versus 82 percent in other industries; third, about 25 percent of the companies responding said they had started new ethics training programs or ethics committees during the past three years.

American firms are acting ethically to improve their public relation image which may help them survive in this competitive environment of business (Brenner, 1992). So, one must understand that business ethics is an integral part of doing business and there is more at stake than market share. Solomon (1994) suggests that ethical codes of conduct should not contradict the "bottom line", but must be, at least, above the "bottom line." Some researchers argue that instrumental ethics (utilitarian view) should not be part of business, and people should be ethical because it is the right thing to do. Others argue that, in reality, ethical behavior will always be instrumental because if it doesn't benefit an individual, then it may have been for the benefit of the group (Carr, 1994). It could be stated that "instrumentality" is a symptom of ethical behavior and should not be the end result of decisions (Wolfe, 1993). Solomon (1994) states that ethical errors end careers more quickly and more definitively than any other mistake in judgment, especially at top layers of management because the harm seems to be greater. To some extent, a well-defined and implemented code of ethics could eliminate some of these problems. It is the executives and top managers who are playing an extremely crucial role in shaping ethical behaviors of everyone in the organization, which will decrease turnover and increase the ethical culture and image of the company (Collins, 1994 & Brenner, 1992).

DeGeorge (1995) states that corporate codes can guide and help the actions of employees on legal matters, conflicts of interest, and help managers and employees to evaluate in ethical terms the firm's ends, practices, and actions, to make sure the firm is following its code and living up to it. In order to improve the organizational practices and ethical behavior, the majority of writers have recommended adopting a corporate code of ethics and forming a high-ranking ethics committee, who could conduct ethics training and monitor periodically the ethical climate of the company. It is also imperative that ethical codes of conduct be enforced to their fullest extent. Davis (1995) states that corporate ethical behavior can be rewarded by increased profits if the consumers evaluate the ethics of the corporation and if the evaluation plays an important role in the consumer's decision whether or not to purchase the corporation's products. Davis confirms, and concludes that good ethics can be good for business. Corporate codes of ethics can be an important tool toward consumer's loyalty and increased profits; and it can and should be measured (Brenner, 1992).

Business Ethics and Corporate Responsibility
There are many corporations beginning to take steps to institutionalize ethics and are creating specific mechanisms and strategies to implement effectively these efforts (Dean, 1992). Almost 90 percent of all business schools are teaching some type of class in ethics (McDonald & Zepp, 1994). Solberg, Strong, and McGuire (1995) suggest that schools should be aware of the values which they are imparting to their graduates. They also emphasize that business ethics topics are extremely important to teach because the majority of undergraduates are in a period of moral transition, seeking to discover a set of ethical standards that is suitable for them. They suggest that values and standards must be discovered by each individual; in other words, values and standards should be owned or self-imposed by the students. They also suggest that ethics instructions should be included in the undergraduate program in a structured system.

There is a hidden cost of about $12 billion per year for American retailers, which is based on consumer and employee shoplifting (Cox et al., 1993). Shoplifting is destructive behavior that is very common among adolescents who are influenced by their friends' behavior, parents' behavior, and their own beliefs about the morality of shoplifting (Cox et al., 1993). There are many companies that invest time, labor, and resources to institute some type of ethical codes or rules to encourage ethical behavior; but they do very little in the actual implementation of these ethical programs (Solberg et al., 1995). Wimbush and Shepard (1994) concluded that higher level managers and supervisors have a significant impact on the organizational climate and implementation of ethical codes and policies for all members. They also state that even when a company does have an ethics policy, members will more likely mimic or act just like their supervisors (Brenner, 1992). As Solberg, Strong, and McGuire (1995) found, ethical values and standards must be learned and cannot be imposed by others. They also suggested that companies should train their high level managers and executives before expecting others to follow ethical values. Hegarty and Sims (1979) found that when a company president wrote a letter to employees reinforcing ethical behavior and warning them of dismissal for non-compliance, the results were an increase in ethical behavior.

McDonald and Zepp (1994) support previous conclusions by stating that ultimately the corporate image is influenced by its member's ethical behavior. They also state that peer influence also affects the corporate image of a company and peer influence varies among cultures. People in different cultures value relationships differently and those values ultimately influence their behavior (Fritzsche, (1995). McDonald and Zepp (1995) stated that the behavior of one's peers had more of an effect in Hong Kong than in the U.S. Peer influences can form the corporate culture of the company, which in turn affects the behavior of each individual (Becker & Fritzsche, 1987). They suggest that if each individual feels as though they are part of the team, then they will have a stronger tendency to conform to the ethical standards of the organization.

Traditional views of corporate moral responsibilities, such as Friedman's profit maximization goal, are being questioned by many organizations; and many organizations agree that good business is "good" for business in the long-run (Becher & Fritzsche, 1987). They also surveyed German, French, and American managers, who all agreed that sound business is good for business. Solomon (1994) concludes that the new corporate world of business needs the return of old traditional values, for example a sense of team and community, integrity, recognition that we are part of a larger world, and the fact that we all stand for something.

DeGeorge (1995) claims that the American people have not played according to a plan in changing the mandate of business. Instead, it has been by legislation, collective bargaining, and the rise in consumerism. He states that the new moral mandate to business can be seen by the movements of consumerism, environmentalism, conservationism, media's coverage of bribery and profit windfalls, and the resulting legislation. Since the service industry is employing more people than factories, and due to the fact that increased wages cannot be covered by an increase in output, the way everyone does business has changed dramatically. DeGeorge states that the new mandate of business is to consider the workers, consumers, the general public, and the shareholder in the making of decisions. The good of all should, and must, be considered because "good" business is good for the company.

The literature of business ethics clearly demonstrates that the business ethics movement seems to be growing; and it is going to be covering complex issues in today's socially responsible global activities. The majority of top executives and managers believe that ethical issues regarding employee safety, environmental issues, and societal issues will be an extremely important part of each company's concerns for years to come. The majority of us are in the service industry, and the satisfaction of associates plays an important role in the survival of organizations. The subject matter of business ethics requires a total company focus and cooperation (Cooke, 1986) between executives, managers, associates and other primary and secondary stakeholders of the institutions or corporations. Business people should live ethics instead of just learning it (Solberg, Strong & McGuire, 1995). Kochunny and Rogers (1994) completed an ethics survey of 728 students and concluded that they found no significant difference between their results and the managers who had been studied previously. This suggests that schools are doing a better job in preparing students for future moral dilemmas which they will be facing.

Business Ethics Research Studies

Baumhart

Baumhart (1961), through *Harvard Business Review*, surveyed 1,700 executives to answer the question: how ethical are businesspeople? Needless to say that Baumhart did not give a final answer, but he found that executives showed a strong desire to improve business behavior. This study also suggested that it is essential for top management to stand its ground and commit itself to making uncompromisingly moral decisions each and every day. Five out of six executives agreed that it is immoral for company executives to act in the interest of shareholders alone and not in the interest of employees and consumers.

This survey used short scenarios and cases to determine executives' attitudes toward ethical issues and problems. These respondents were divided into two groups; one answered what they would do in an ethical situation, while the other group answered what the average business executive would do in an ethical situation. This study concluded, consistently with other recent studies, that executives rated themselves more ethical than other executives. Executives were aware of the social responsibilities of the business and they saw the corporation as a human society, which is a subset of the larger society in which it functions. In some cases, the executives disagreed on ethical situations and about twenty-five percent could not recognize an ethical situation. These executives suggested that a man is most likely to act ethically if he has a well-defined code of ethics. Also, if his superiors are highly ethical, then he could be expected to be consistently ethical. Executives revealed that there are many pressures for unethical conduct because there are many economic solutions which conflict with ethical standards.

Almost all executives, ninety-nine percent, agreed that sound ethics is good business in the long-run. However, they believe that ethical behavior starts at the top and must be enforced and shown by example each and every day. They suggested that a code of ethics for the industry would be helpful if it has "teeth," that is, it is capable of enforcement. The executives also suggested that group discussions of day-to-day moral situations and alternatives, as well as implications, should be conducted with businesspeople.

Baumhart's study has been replicated by Brenner and Molander (1977), Glenn (1990), as well as Vitell and Festervand in (1987), all of which generally supported the original findings. People still rated others to be less ethical than themselves; and Vitell and Festervand's (1987) survey showed that people would make more unethical decisions than the previous studies. They also concluded that more business people would make an unethical decision if it was in the best interest of company and increased profits, as well as the fact that young people would "play" closer to ethical margins than older people. Glenn (1990) used Baumhart's original questions to survey graduate and undergraduate students. He concluded that students and their professors view ethics much less relevant in school curriculum than practicing managers. He found that 87.5 percent of managers said "yes" to a separate ethics course being taught in school curriculum, compared to only 53 percent of students who thought a separate ethics course should be taught in a degree program. Glenn also concluded that schools should stress ethical behavior to students, starting with the admissions process. He found that schools with the lowest reported rates of cheating require applicants to write an essay on ethics during the admissions process. Glen (1990) concluded that there were very little differences in responses of students in this survey and those of businesspeople in 1961. Students, as well as practicing managers and executives, agree that one's personal code of behavior is the most influential factor in moral decision-making.

Arlow and Ulrich

Arlow and Ulrich (1980) used Clark's instrument to survey 120 undergraduate students in the fields of accounting, business management, and marketing, who had enrolled in "business and society" courses. The students were given a test at the beginning of the course and again at the end of the course in order to examine the effects of the class on their moral decision-making. The results for Personal Business Ethics Scores (PBES) showed that there were significant differences in their responses based on the student's major. The accounting students started with a high score, and at the post-test their scores decreased to some extent, while the marketing and management student's scores increased at the post-test. The results for the Social Responsibility Scores (SRS) suggested that the marketing and management students showed a greater awareness of the social responsibility issues than accounting students. Overall, they concluded that students have lower personal business ethics than executives and managers who were surveyed in Clark's survey. They further stated that business students in this study did not seem to represent a new source of business ethics.

Four years later, Arlow and Ulirch (1985) surveyed those students from their 1980 survey to see if actual industry experience had affected their business ethics. They were able to reach 110 of the original participants and 73 responded and were used for the results of this longitudinal study. They concluded that there is no long-term effect, based on their study, of teaching business ethics to undergraduate business students in a business and society course.

George Stevens

In 1984, George E. Stevens used Clark's instrument to survey 113 business executive (95 male and 18 females) and 349 business students (198 males and 151 females). He wanted to find out the responses of current and future managers (students) regarding their business ethics and social responsibility. His results showed that executives scored higher than the business students on the PBES and just slightly higher on the SRS. A study by Harris and Sutton (1995) concluded that students may not be less moral than executives. However, students were shown to be more tolerant of behaviors relating to specific domains of ethical judgments than more experienced managers and executives (Harris & Sutton, 1995). Steven's study suggested that there was no evidence of the students representing a new source of business ethics. Stevens also analyzed the data based on students' race, sex, and status (graduate vs. undergraduate) and found only minor differences.

Wynd and Mager

Wynd and Mager (1989) completed a study on whether "business and society" courses can affect ethical behavior of students or not. They collected data from students for over two years by using Clark's (1966) instrument and conducted a pre and post class survey. They concluded that the "business and society" class had no impact on Personal Business Ethics Scores and Social Responsibility Scores of students who had completed the class. Glenn (1992) completed a pre and post survey of 460 students to find if a "business and society" course can affect ethical judgment of future managers. Glenn concluded that students can move toward a more moral direction as a result of completing a "business and society" course.

Stephenson, Galbraith, and Grimm

Stephenson, Galbraith, and Grimm (1995) used Clark's instrument to investigate the perception of five constituent groups of an accredited business school to determine their perceptions of others' ethics, of their own ethics and ideal values, and of how business ethics can be improved. There were 106 graduating seniors, 65 MBA students, 28 small business clients, 18 school of Business and Economics Advisory Board respondents, and 22 faculty members from School of Business and Economics. The respondents were requested to assess what the person in the scenario would do, what the respondent him/herself would do, and what the person felt he/she should do.

They concluded that over half of the constituents believed the decision maker would make the immoral decision; and the results support previous findings (Ford & Richardson, 1994; Baumhart, 1961) that individuals perceive themselves to be more moral than others. The constituent respondent is more moral but still not as moral as he/she thought or felt that he/she should be. Business students expressed the lowest ethics out of all the constituents in the sample. A majority of the constituents agreed more on what should be done in each situation than they judged they would do in a given situation. All constituents supported and agreed to proposals to improve ethics by developing principles of business ethics, ethics courses in business schools, and by introducing industry codes of ethics. It was also suggested that businesses should go well above and beyond reviewing codes of conduct or training to facilitate ethical behavior among employees. They suggest that peer training, and emphasis as well as demonstrating the positive impact of ethical behavior on the bottom line could encourage ethical behavior (Badenhorst, 1994). The attitude of executives toward ethical issues seems to have a major influence on the ethical behavior of each individual in the corporation (Murphy, Smith & Daley, 1992).

Clark's Survey of Executives and Students

John W. Clark, Columbian Economist, surveyed 103 executives and top managers to investigate "contemporary" business ethics. Clark created scenarios which represented common day-to-day business issues and asked the respondents to approve or disapprove with each decision made in the scenario. The respondents would answer "somewhat approve" or "approve" if they approve of the decision; and if they did not approve, they would respond "somewhat disapprove" or "disapprove." This was based on the Likert's scale of 1 (approve) to 5 (disapprove) and 3 being the mid-point or no opinion. This type of questioning, according to Clark and Baumhart, does not put a person in the position of approving or not approving an immoral act. People, in general, do not want to provide answers that might make them look immoral. So approving or not approving the decision made in the case would allow them to support either a personal gain, a corporate gain or a wider social position.

Clark (1966) created two ethical scales, the Personal Business Ethics Scale (PBES) and the Social Responsibility Scales (SRS). The Personal Business Ethics Scale measures a person's commitment to integrity, honesty, and observance of the laws regulating business decisions; and the Social Responsibility Scale measures the degree to which a person considers oneself morally responsible for the welfare of others including everyone in the society and the society as well. There were eleven scenarios for the PBES and seven scenarios for the SRS. The results for PBES can range from a minimum of 11 (approving) to maximum of 55 (disapproving). The results for the SRS can range from a low of 7 (disapproving) to a high score of 35 (approving), representing a high level of social responsibility to the society. Clark's PBES results' showed an average score of 43, which means that most people did not approve of the decisions, and leaned toward the social values by sacrificing personal gain. The average score for SRS's were 21, which means that about half of them leaned toward serving the community's interest by performing one's duties in the most efficient way possible.

Research Conclusions

There are many authors researching the development of moral behaviors in individuals based on experience, education, sex, and maturity level/age. Most of the researchers support the fact that education and experience have a positive effect on the moral development of individuals. There are many sources of ethical/moral values and they are all very important to one's behavior. Family, peers, institutions, and the media are important sources of moral/ethical values. In the business sector, the professional role models and company policies are the major determinants of how individuals will behave. Employees' ethical/moral behavior is greatly influenced by their perception of organizational policies and practices, which constitute an ethical climate (Wimbush & Shepard, 1994). Moral commitments to the future of a firm will ensure efforts that are both cooperative and innovative. Also, cooperative, innovative, and morally directed behaviors on the part of all of the stakeholder groups can lead to a competitive and successful firm over time (Quinn & Jones, 1995).

Most researchers of ethics suggest that moral/ethical teachings should be incorporated in the school curriculum; and they tend to agree that all courses should have some type of emphasis on ethics and morality (Brown, 1994). Business ethics instructions are important because most undergraduates are in a stage of moral transition, trying to gather standards of ethical behavior which might be suitable for them (Solberg et al., 1995).

Business ethics is concerned with the mission of the firm, how it is accomplished, and the consequences it may have to the society in general. According to Solomon (1994), we always should follow the "*three Cs*" of business. They are the need for *compliance* with the rules, *contributions* which business can make to the society, and the *consequences* of business activity. There are five key areas which corporate ethics should be concerned with and they are: employees want fairness, consumers would like to have quality, suppliers count on dependability, managers tend to value trustworthiness, and the community would like to see responsibility and accountability (Solomon, 1994).

There are many stakeholders that a firm could have; and their trust, commitment, and efforts are as essential to the success of the firm as are the competitive advantages and strategic positions of its planning process (Hosmer, 1994). Some researchers of ethics suggest that ethics should be incorporated in the school curriculum, and they tend to agree that all courses should have some type of emphasis on ethics. Brown (1994) and other researchers state that the immediate concern is to find effective methods of incorporating ethics into the heart of business education. Researchers suggest we should use role-playing, discussions of newspaper articles and other current media issues in academic courses to help students be more practical so they can deal more effectively with actual situations.

Summary

As individuals grow old and gain more experience, their level of moral and ethical standard develops and becomes more sophisticated. Individual moral development starts at a young age and continues until adulthood and beyond. It could even extend to the late thirties, even forties and beyond. Individuals develop differently based on their experiences and education, as well as societal knowledge. Males and females move differently through the stages of moral development and each person could be at different levels of ethical maturity at different times in their lives. Business people also develop ethical maturity as they gain more experience based on their work, social interaction, and educational sessions. Society demands that business people be more aware of the social implications of their decisions and to make sure that the social welfare of society takes precedence over the profit-maximization goal.

Based on the literature review of managers and executives, it is clear that older managers seem to be more ethical than younger managers. This is probably due to their awareness of the larger social implications which their decisions could impact. The research herein is based on a study of business ethics of managers in the supermarket industry. Supermarket managers can be very influential on our youth. The majority of students and young people work part-time or full-time in supermarkets, and most likely this would be their first work experience in the "real world" of business. Supermarket managers and associates work in the service industry, and their ethical values and moral judgments could have a great impact on the organization.

This chapter provided some of the common definitions for major terms used in ethics research. Since the terms values, ethics and morals are often used interchangeably by authors and practitioners, the following practical definitions are highlighted here for differentiation and a quick review:

- *Values* are core, self-chosen beliefs or desires that guide or motivate one's attitude and actions. What one values drives his/her behavior. Some people value honesty or truthfulness in all situations while others value loyalty to colleagues. Some people value life in all of its forms while others limit it to an extent. Research has shown that one of the most important indicators of attitudes and behavior is value structures, because values are the underlying structures that affect attitudes and subsequent behavior.
- *Ethics* is the branch of philosophy that theoretically, logically, and rationally determines right from wrong, good from bad, moral from immoral, and just from unjust actions, conducts, and behaviors. Some people define ethics as *doing what you say you would do* or *walking the talk*.
- *Morals* are judgments, standards, and rules of good conduct in the society. They guide people toward permissible behavior with regard to basic values.

Overall, this study examines the ethical responses of supermarket managers and employees to determine whether age, management experience, education, and gender are factors in ethical evaluation and moral decision-making. The next chapter presents the research design and methodology of this study.

III – RESEARCH METHODOLOGY

This chapter defines the research design and methodology for this study on business ethics in a retail setting. More specifically, it describes the corresponding population and sample, the research variables and relationship of variables, survey instruments, reliability and validity, data collection procedure, research questions with their respective hypotheses, data analysis, and general strategy of the study.

Introduction

There is sufficient evidence that managers have a significant impact on the organizational climate and behavior of their subordinates (Wimbush & Shepard, 1994). These managers are involved in making moral decisions that affect their people and the profitability of their companies. In order to recognize ethical situations and make moral decisions, individuals must have a high level of moral maturity. Based on the cognitive moral development theory of Kohlberg (1981), moral maturity occurs in stages; and some individuals may not reach their highest level of moral maturity until the early to late thirties.

Research on the business ethics of managers and students indicates that students have lower business ethics scores than managers (Stephenson et al., 1995; Arlow & Ulrich, 1980). Stephenson et al. (1995), Stevens (1984), Arlow (1991), and Arlow and Ulrich (1980, 1985, 1988) used Clark's (1966) instrument to study business ethics of managers and students. Stephenson et al. (1995) concluded that undergraduate students tended to have the lowest estimation of others' ethics and the least self-described ethical behavior compared to other constituent groups. They also concluded that believing others are less ethical actually, may encourage less ethical behavior. Arlow and Ulrich (1980, 1985, and 1988) found differences among students based on their academic majors; and Peter Arlow (1991) concluded that business students are no less ethical than non-business students. Stevens (1984) found that business ethics scores of students were lower than executives; however, both students and executives had similar scores on social responsibility tests. Studies using Clark's (1966) instrument reported that students are less ethical than managers. Neither study used Supermarket managers and employees.

The author posits that Supermarket employees who are under the age necessary for moral maturity and who have no supermarket management experience will have lower ethical scores than Supermarket managers and executives. This research, using Clark's (1966) instrument, compares the Personal Business Ethics Scores (PBES) of Supermarket employees/students who are 25 years of age or younger and have no management experience, with the scores of managers of Supermarkets, who are 26 years of age or older and have five years of management experience. The purpose of this research is to determine whether management experience gained through the maturation process plays a role in ethical decision-making. This research also considers gender and education as factors which may account for differences between both employees and managers.

Statement of the Problem

There have been several studies that link the moral and immoral behavior of individuals to their experience, age, gender, and maturity levels. Researchers (i.e., Kohlberg, Piaget, Clark) have concluded that as individuals mature (grow older and acquire experience), their ethical values and behaviors tend to improve. This growth in the moral development of individuals takes place from early childhood until the late twenties and thirties.

The *research question* to be answered is: Would age, gender, education, and management experience affect the moral development of individuals in the retail environment? Of course, the assumed moderating variable is that the person is working in a values-focused environment where the organizational culture encourages everyone to do what is right for their customers, employees, suppliers and other relevant stakeholders. As demonstrated in Figure 2, the *dependent variable* is "Moral Maturity" levels or moral development levels of respondents. The *independent variables* affecting one's moral development (maturity) are age, gender, management experience, and education.

Figure 2 - The Ethical Maturity Model

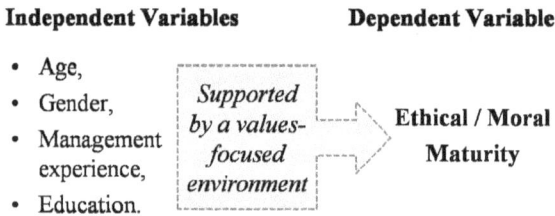

This study uses Clark's (1966) instrument to compare the results of Personal Business Ethics Scores (PBES) of Supermarket managers, who have at least five years of management experience and are at least 26 years old, with supermarket employees who are 25 years old or younger and who have no formal management experience. The comparisons are based on age, supermarket management experience, education, and gender. Again, the research question to be answered is whether age, gender, education, and management experience affect the moral development of individuals. The independent variables affecting one's moral development are age, gender, management experience, and education. The specific hypotheses, as previously stated, are as follows:

1. *Null Hypothesis I* - Individuals who are 25 years old or younger will have Personal Business Ethics Scores (PBES) that are equivalent to or greater than those individuals who are 26 years of age or older.
2. *Null Hypothesis II* - Females who are 25 years old or younger will have Personal Business Ethics Scores that are equivalent to or greater than males who are 25 years of age or younger.
3. *Null Hypothesis III* - Females who are 26 years of age or older will have Personal Business Ethics Scores that are equivalent to or greater than males who are 26 years of age or older.
4. *Null Hypothesis IV* - Individuals who have five or more years of supermarket management experience will have Personal Business Ethics Scores that are equivalent to or greater than individuals who do not have any management experience at all.
5. *Null Hypothesis V* - Females who have five or more years of supermarket management experience will have Personal Business Ethics Scores that are equivalent to or greater than males who have five or more years of supermarket management experience.
6. *Null Hypothesis VI* - Females with no management experience will have Personal Business Ethics Scores that are equivalent to or greater than males who have no management experience.
7. *Null Hypothesis VII* - Individuals who have four or more years of formal college education will have Personal Business Ethics Scores that are equivalent to or greater than individuals who do not have any formal college education.

Population and Sampling Method
Survey research techniques have been successfully used to study the values and beliefs of people in the organizational culture and environment. The analytical survey method of research has many advantages when compared to other available methods. "The accuracy of properly drawn samples is frequently surprising, even to the experts in the field…A sample of 600 to 700 individuals or families can give a remarkably accurate portrait of a community--its values, attitudes, and beliefs" (Kerlinger, 1986, p. 387).

When using self-administered questionnaires, the errors associated with interviewer subjectivity is totally eliminated. The self-administered questionnaires also offer greater anonymity, which can be extremely important when conducting research in the area of ethics. Respondents are asked questions that are very personal in nature because they deal with their values, beliefs, and daily practices. Also, the self-administered questionnaires allow the researcher to objectively analyze the data and discover statistically significant relationships.

This study targeted employees and managers of a Fortune One Hundred firm with more than 100,000 employees in the supermarket industry and growing rapidly. The host company has been voted to be one of the hundred best companies to work for in America by Robert Levering and Milton Moskowitz in their 1994 book, titled *"The 100 Best Companies To Work For In America."* This research study of retail employees compares employees who were under 26 years of age and who have not worked in any management position with managers who are at least 26 years of age and have had five or more years of supermarket management experience. According to Kohlberg's (1981) and Liebert's (1984) study, these employees will not have reached the level of moral maturity or sophistication that can be evidenced in individuals who are 26 years of age or older and have had five years of management experience.

The surveys were sent to Supermarket employees and managers in the Florida region. A paragraph explaining the purpose of this research and guaranteeing total confidentiality was included with each survey. Twelve hundred questionnaires were sent to Supermarket employees and managers who were asked to voluntarily complete the questionnaire during their regular shift and return it to the author by company mail. Six hundred surveys were sent to management and six hundred were sent to non-management.

A total of 635 surveys, comprising a response rate of 53 percent, were returned. From the returned surveys, a total of 33 surveys were incomplete and could not be used. A total of 602 surveys were left to conduct this survey and 385 of them (64%) represent people who have been working with this company for at least six years or more. Twenty percent (n=121) of these respondents are 25 years of age or younger. A total of 275 managers and assistant managers, 46% of the respondents, participated in this survey; and only 165 of them (60%) have six or more years of management experience in the supermarket industry and are 26 years of age or older. The respondents are 51.5% (n=310) males and 48.5% (n=292) females. From the total sample, 350 (58%) people have twelve years of education or less, and 52 (9%) people have four or more years of college education. A majority of the respondents, 329 individuals, are from the grocery department, six respondents are from the pharmacy department, and the rest of the respondents are equally divided into the bakery (67), meat (66), deli (66), and produce (68) departments.

Instrument

Researchers have been trying to create the best method of obtaining true information from respondents, without making them feel guilty or putting them in a position where they would have to state what they would do in each situation. To do this most effectively, the majority of researchers (for example, Baumhart, 1961; Clark, 1966) have agreed that scenarios are a convenient method of measuring the respondent's approval or disapproval of each situation, without requiring them to state what they themselves would do in each situation by themselves. Social research often requires that people reveal personal information about themselves which might be unknown to their closest friends and family members (Babbie, 1992); and this is not always an easy task.

Clark's 1966 questionnaire was used for this research; and this questionnaire is based on prior research conducted in the field of business ethics. This instrument contains eleven short scenarios dealing with specific moral situations. These scenarios were used by Clark to determine the Personal Business Ethics Scores of managers and students. Table 1.0 lists a general outline of the scenarios. The questionnaire used for this study can be found in the Appendix section of this book.

The Personal Business Ethics Scores (PBES) measures one's level of commitment to personal integrity and honesty in business decisions and to the laws governing business (Arlow & Ulrich, 1980). The scores derived from the scenarios are measured on a Likert five point scale, 1 (strongly approve) to 5 (strongly disapprove). The PBES totals for the eleven scenarios could range from a low score of 11 to a high score of 55. The low score represents a low sense of personal business ethics; and a high score represents a high sense of personal business ethics.

TABLE 1 - CLARK'S PBES SCENARIOS

1. Electrical-equipment price conspiracy
2. Conflict with superior's ethics
3. Insider information of stock split
4. Sharp selling of used cars
5. Use of inferior products
6. Padding the expense account
7. Promotion of less capable based on connections
8. Pressure in newspaper for advertising
9. Auditor overlooks a bribe
10. Pirating employees to learn competitors' secrets
11. Recommending questionable bonds

The original Clark instrument was written in the 1960s. Certain details of the scenarios have been updated by past researchers (for example, Arlow & Ulrich, 1980; Stevens, 1984; Wynd & Mager, 1989; Freedman, 1990; Stephenson et al., 1995) to accurately reflect today's conditions. For example, scenario six deals with padding an expense account. The dollar values were changed from a salary of $12,000 per year, and the padding of the expense account by $600, to a salary of $36,000 per year, and $1,800 "padding", which maintain the original 5% padding amount. According to Freedman (1990), this revision has been verified by the original author, Clark; and it is still valid and reliable. All moral scenarios are relevant to the business dealings of individuals and companies in the current environment. Topics such as making illegal payments, insider trading, nepotism or favoritism to certain individuals during promotions, selling inferior products, and environmental issues are the topics of daily newspaper and television discussions. Some of these issues are national; yet others are international and thus can affect everyone in the world. AT&T, for example, eliminated about 40,000 jobs over a three-year period (Arnst, 1996). It has been predicted that the telecommunication industry eliminated close to 100,000 jobs over a five-year period; and this reduction in force, which has only grown due to the recent recession in the U.S., involves many ethical decisions on the part of company executives and senior managers eliminating jobs. It appears as though nepotism, love of personal power and gain, tribalism, and other bribery evils are universal situations representing unfair practices. Individuals, logical and realistic human beings, desiring to keep their jobs and their friends, may deviate from their moral standards to conform with the pressures of society. The dilemmas in this survey are relevant to such practices; and the survey thus measures the respondents' level of commitment to personal integrity in such situations as well as their observance of the laws governing business.

Validity and Reliability of the Instrument

This questionnaire was presented by its creator (Clark, 1966) to a panel of five faculty members, in the marketing department, at University of Southern California. These faculty members concluded that the scenarios were valid for the two scales. A standard test-retest reliability check was made of each of the two scales. The test was twice administered to a group of 40 subjects with a three-week interval between test administrations. The test-retest reliability coefficient for the PBES was .76, which manifests an acceptable degree of reliability. The test-retest reliability coefficient for the SRS was .86, which represents a high degree of reliability (Clark, 1966).

Data Analysis Method

This questionnaire consists of eleven questions which represent the Personal Business Ethics Scores (PBES). The PBES represents a score between 11, indicating low personal business ethics, to 55, indicating very high personal business ethics. An analysis of variance (ANOVA) at the $p < .05$ level of significance is used to determine if there are differences in the responses of Supermarket employees who are 25 years old or younger and have no management experience, with those of Supermarket managers who have five or more years of management experience and are at least twenty six years old. The .05 level of significance has been chosen because it is an appropriate level of significance for most social science research (Freedman, 1990; Babbie, 1992).

Analysis of variance (ANOVA) has been suggested to be used for such research; and Kerlinger (1986, pp. 265-270) lists four assumptions to consider when selecting a parametric statistical test, which are:

1. Normality -- the samples should be drawn from a population that is normally distributed.
2. Homogeneity of variance -- variances should be homogeneous from group to group with boundaries.
3. The measure analyzed should be continuous containing equal intervals.
4. Each observation should be independent.

Assumptions and Limitations

The assumption is made that the data collection method will be appropriate for the retail sample population being studied and the respondents will be honest in their responses. Since the study is voluntary and no names are recorded, it is reasonable to assume that the responses are honest. This study is limited to retail employees and managers of a large Fortune 100 firm. Assumptions are made by the researcher that the responses will be of use in making generalities regarding the relationship between ethical maturity and demographic variables including age, gender, education, and management experience. Conclusions drawn from the results of this study will be reflective of the limitations presented.

Summary

Chapter III presented the research design and methodology of the study including the corresponding population and sample, the research variables and relationship of variables, survey instruments, reliability and validity, data collection procedure, research questions with their respective hypotheses, data analysis and strategy, and the limitations of the study. The study's research questions and hypotheses are tested and discussed in Chapter IV.

CHAPTER FOUR

IV – ANALYSIS AND RESULTS

This chapter presents the results of analyzed data from the hypotheses developed in chapter III. The purpose of this study was to examine the relationship between age, gender, education, and management experience with ethical maturity in a retail setting. The following sections present demographics of the sample population, analysis of the reported data, and the results of hypothesis tests.

Introduction and Analysis

The findings reported in this chapter are developed using primary data collected from supermarket managers and employees. This study used a structured survey, developed by Clark (1966), to compare the Personal Business Ethics Scores (PBES) of supermarket employees and managers based on their age, supermarket management experience, education, and gender. The PBES determines one's degree of commitment to personal integrity and honesty in business situations as well as to the observance of the laws governing business.

The Personal Business Ethics Scores (PBES) survey contains short scenarios that represent the actions of one or more individuals in a given situation. The respondents were asked to show their agreement or disagreement based on a Likert 5-point scale. In this scale, a response of strongly agree is given a score of 1, and a response of strongly disagree is given a score of 5. Each individual's total score can range from a low of 11, representing a low score of personal business ethics, to a high of 55, reflecting a high score of personal business ethics. Responses to the eleven short scenarios measure one's level of commitment to personal integrity and honesty in the given business situations. These scenarios also measure one's level of commitment to the observance of the laws governing business.

An analysis of variance (ANOVA) at the .05 level of significance is used to test the hypothesis representing its significance at the 95% confidence interval.

ANOVA is an appropriate method of testing survey results for statistically significant differences (Kerlinger, 1986). The .05 level of significance has been chosen because it is an appropriate level of significance for most social science research (Freedman, 1990; Babbie, 1992).

Demographic Data

A total of 1,200 surveys were sent to employees and managers of the targeted supermarket in the Florida district by Disney World. A total of 635 surveys, comprising a response rate of 53 percent, were returned. This high return rate can be attributed to the host company's encouragement that their employees complete the survey during their work hours. From the returned surveys, a total of 33 surveys were incomplete and could not be used. A total of 602 surveys were left for analysis; and 385 of them (64%) represent people who have been working with this company for at least six years or more. Twenty percent (n=121) of these respondents are 25 years of age or younger. A total of 275 managers and assistant managers, 46% of the respondents, participated in this survey, and only 165 of them (60%) have six or more years of management experience in the supermarket industry and are 26 years of age or older. From the total of 165 managers with six or more years of supermarket management experience, only 19 are females, and 146 are males. The gender distribution of survey respondents are 51.5% (n=310) males and 48.5% (n=292) females. From the total sample, 350 (58%) individuals have twelve years of education or less, and 52 (9%) individuals have four or more years of formal college education.

The majority of the respondents, 329 individuals, are from the grocery department, six individuals are from the pharmacy department, and the rest of the respondents are equally divided into the bakery (67), meat (66), deli (66), and produce (68) departments.

Test of the Hypotheses

This study used the SPSS software program as a database and used the ANOVA section to evaluate each hypothesis at the specified level (5%) of significance. The following pages, tables and explanations are geared toward each hypothesis and its explanation.

Hypothesis I

Null hypothesis I states that individuals who are 25 years of age or younger (X_1) will have Personal Business Ethics Scores (PBES) that are equivalent to or greater than those individuals who are 26 years of age or older (X_2). The alternative hypothesis states that individuals who are 25 years of age or younger will have PBES that are lower than those individuals who are 26 years of age or older.

$$Ho: X_1 \geq X_2$$
$$H_1: X_1 < X_2$$

ANOVA at a 5% level of significance was used to test the null hypothesis. Table 1.1 shows the results of the ANOVA test. The PBES mean of individuals 25 years of age or younger is 42.07, and the PBES mean for individuals 26 years of age or older is 44.98, with an F-value of 21.53 at a level of significance of .000. The results indicate that the PBES mean value for individuals 26 years of age or older is significantly higher than the PBES value for individuals 25 years of age or younger. Null Hypothesis I was rejected and the alternate hypothesis was supported, respondents 25 years of age and younger had lower PBES scores than those who were 26 years of age or older.

This result is consistent with previous research and supports the moral development theory that age is a factor in moral development. People who are 26 years of age or older are at a higher level of moral development than individuals who are 25 years of age or younger. These findings suggest that individuals can develop moral maturity or sophistication as they become older. This result supports Jadack's (1995) doctoral dissertation study from the Department of Psychology and the School of Nursing at the University of Wisconsin - Madison. Using Kohlberg's moral stage theory and Gilligan's moral orientation model, Jadack concluded that older population in her sample had a significantly higher stage of moral reasoning than the younger age group when responding to dilemmas about sexually transmitted diseases.

Table 1.1 - ANALYSIS OF VARIANCE AND MEAN VALUES

Source	Sum of Squares	DF	Mean Squares	F	Significance of F
Main Effects	8222.78	1	822.78	21.53	.000
	8222.78	1	822.78	21.53	.000
Explained	8222.78	1	822.78	21.53	.000
Residual	22933.34	600	38.22		
Total	23756.11	601			

Total Sample Population   N = 602
25 years and younger n = 121 $X_1 = 42.07$
26 years and older   n = 481 $X_2 = 44.98$

DF = Degrees of freedom. One fewer than the number of categories. Mean Squares = Sum of squares divided by degrees of freedom. F = Residual value divided by the Mean Squares.
Signif of F = Significance of F is the actual level of significance for this test that is compared to the level of significance that is required to test the null hypothesis. If the Significance of F value is less than .05, the null hypothesis is rejected. Source: Norusis, SPSS/PC + Base Manual.

Hypothesis II

Null hypothesis II states that females who are 25 years of age or younger will (X_1) have Personal Business Ethics Scores (PBES) that are equivalent to or greater than males who are 25 years of age or younger (X_2). The alternative hypothesis states that females who are 25 years of age or younger will have PBES that are lower than males who are 25 years of age or younger.

$$Ho: \ X_1 \geq X_2$$
$$H_1: \ X_1 < X_2$$

ANOVA at a 5% level of significance was used to test the null hypothesis. Table 2 shows the results of the ANOVA test. The PBES mean of females 25 years of age or younger is 42.78, and the PBES mean for males 25 years of age or younger is 40.94, with an F-value of 2.35 at a level of significance of .128. The results indicate that there is no significant difference in the PBES mean value of female and male employees 25 years old or younger. Null hypothesis II failed to be rejected.

Although the PBES mean of females who are 25 years of age or younger is higher than males who are 25 years of age or younger, it is not significantly higher. The result does not support the moral development theory that gender is a factor in moral development of individuals who are 25 years of age or younger.

Table 2 - ANALYSIS OF VARIANCE AND MEAN VALUES

Source	Sum of Squares	DF	Mean Squares	F	Significance of F
Main Effects	98.12	1	98.12	2.35	.128
	98.12	1	98.12	2.35	.128
Explained	98.12	1	98.12	2.35	.128
Residual	4969.35	119	41.76		
Total	5067.47	120			

Total Sample Population   N = 121
Males 25 years and younger   n = 47 $X_2 = 40.94$
Females 25 years and younger   n = 74 $X_1 = 42.78$

Hypothesis III

Null Hypothesis III states that females who are 26 years of age or older (X_1) will have Personal Business Ethics Scores that are equivalent to or greater than males who are 26 years of age or older (X_2). The alternate hypothesis states that females who are 26 years of age or older will have Personal Business Ethics Scores that are lower than males who are 26 years of age or older.

$$Ho: \ X_1 \geq X_2$$
$$H_1: \ X_1 < X_2$$

ANOVA at a 5% level of significance was used to test the null hypothesis. Table 3 shows the results of the ANOVA test. The PBES mean of females 26 years of age and older is 45.29, and the PBES of males 25 years of age and older is 44.73, with an F-value 1.03 at a level of significance of .310. The results indicate that there is no significant difference in the PBES mean value of females and males who are 26 years of age and older. Null hypothesis III failed to be rejected.

The result does not support moral development theory that gender is a factor in the moral development of individuals who are 26 years of age or older. Although the PBES mean of females who are at least 26 years of age or older is higher than males who are at least 26 years of age or older, the difference is not significant.

Table 3 - ANALYSIS OF VARIANCE AND MEAN VALUES

Source	Sum of Squares	DF	Mean Squares	F	Significance of F
Main Effects	38.37	1	38.37	1.03	.310
	38.37	1	38.37	1.03	.310
Explained	38.37	1	38.37	1.03	.310
Residual	17827.50	479	37.22		
Total	17865.87	480			

Total Sample Population N = 481
Males 26 years and older n = 263 $X_2 = 44.73$
Females 26 years and older n = 218 $X_1 = 45.29$

Hypothesis IV

Null hypothesis IV states that individuals who have five or more years of supermarket management experience (X_1) will have Personal Business Ethics Scores (PBES) that are equivalent to or greater than individuals who do not have any management experience at all (X_2). The alternative hypothesis states that individuals who have five or more years of supermarket management experience will have PBESs that are lower than those individuals with no management experience.

$$Ho: \ X_1 \geq X_2$$
$$H_1: \ X_1 < X_2$$

ANOVA at a 5% level of significance was used to test the null hypothesis. Table 4 shows the results of the ANOVA test. The PBES mean of individuals with five or more years of supermarket management experience is 45.25, and the PBES mean for individuals with no management experience is 43.62, with an F-value of 6.94 at a level of significance of .009.

Table 4 - ANALYSIS OF VARIANCE AND MEAN VALUES

Source	Sum of Squares	DF	Mean Squares	F	Significance of F
Main Effects	269.07	1	269.07	6.94	.009
	269.07	1	269.07	6.94	.009
Explained	269.07	1	269.07	6.94	.009
Residual	16217.65	418	38.80		
Total	16486.71	419			

Total Sample Population N = 420
5 or more years of management experience, n = 165 $X_1 = 45.25$
No management experience, n = 255 $X_2 = 43.62$

The results indicate that the PBES mean value for individuals with five or more years of supermarket management experience is significantly higher than the PBES value for individuals with no supermarket management experience. Null Hypothesis IV failed to be rejected. This result supports moral development theory that management experience is a factor in moral maturity.

Hypothesis V

Null Hypothesis V states that females who have five or more years of supermarket management experience (X_1) will have Personal Business Ethics Scores that are equivalent to or greater than males who have five or more years of supermarket management experience (X_2). The alternate hypothesis states that females who have five or more years of supermarket management experience will have Personal Business Ethics Scores that are lower than males who have five or more years of supermarket management experience.

$$Ho: \ X_1 \geq X_2$$
$$H_1: \ X_1 < X_2$$

ANOVA at a 5% level of significance was used to test the null hypothesis. Table 5 shows the results of the ANOVA test. The PBES mean of females with five or more years of supermarket management experience is 46.42, and the PBES mean for males with five or more years of supermarket management experience is 45.10, with an F-value of .755 at a level of significance of .386. The ANOVA in table 5 indicates that there are no significant differences between PBES mean value of females with five or more years of management experience and males with five or more years of experience. The null hypothesis failed to be rejected. This result does not support moral development theory that gender is a factor in moral development.

Table 5 - ANALYSIS OF VARIANCE AND MEAN VALUES

Source	Sum of Squares	DF	Mean Squares	F	Significance of F
Main Effects	29.22	1	29.22	.755	.386
	29.22	1	29.22	.755	.386
Explained	29.22	1	29.22	.755	.386
Residual	6308.09	163	38.70		
Total	6337.31	164			

Total Sample Population N = 165
Males 5 or more years of management experience   n = 146 $X_2 = 45.10$
Females 5 or more years of management experience n = 19 $X_1 = 46.42$

Hypothesis VI

Null Hypothesis VI states that females with no management experience (X_1) will have Personal Business Ethics Scores that are equivalent to or greater than males who have no management experience (X_2). The alternate hypothesis VI states that females with no management experience will have Personal Business Ethics Scores that are lower than males who have no management experience.

$$\text{Ho:} \quad X_1 \geq X_2$$
$$H_1: \quad X_1 < X_2$$

ANOVA at a 5% level of significance was used to test the null hypothesis. Table 6 shows the results of the ANOVA test. The PBES mean of females with no management experience is 44.22, and the PBES for males with no management experience is 41.86, with an F-value of 7.07 at a level of significance of .008. The ANOVA indicates that there are significant differences between these two groups. Females with no management experience have a significantly higher mean PBES value than males with no management experience. The null hypothesis VI failed to be rejected.

This result supports the moral development theory that gender is a factor in moral development; however, it is only true in the case of individuals with no management experience. It also supports Carol Gilligan's view that the ethical values of females are higher than those of males.

Table 6 - ANALYSIS OF VARIANCE AND MEAN VALUES

Source	Sum of Squares	DF	Mean Squares	F	Significance of F
Main Effects	268.43	1	268.43	7.07	.008
	268.43	1	268.43	7.07	.008
Explained	268.43	1	268.43	7.07	.008
Residual	9611.91	253	37.99		
Total	9880.34	254			

Total Sample Population N = 255
Males with no management experience   n = 65 $X_2 = 41.86$
Females with no management experience n = 190 $X_1 = 44.22$

Hypothesis VII

Null hypothesis VII states that individuals who have four or more years of formal college education (X_1) will have Personal Business Ethics Scores (PBES) that are equivalent to or greater than individuals who do not have any formal college education (X_2). The alternative hypothesis states that individuals who have four or more years of formal college education will have lower PBESs than those individuals who do not have any formal college education.

$$\text{Ho:} \quad X_1 \geq X_2$$
$$H_1: \quad X_1 < X_2$$

ANOVA at a 5% level of significance was used to test the null hypothesis. Table 7 shows the results of the ANOVA test. The PBES mean of individuals who have four or more years of formal college education is 45.81, and the PBES mean for individuals who do not have any formal college education is 44.33, with an F-value of 2.64 at a level of significance of .105. The results indicate that there is no significant difference in the PBES mean value of individuals who have four or more years of formal college education and those that do not have any formal college education. Null hypothesis VII failed to be rejected. This result does not support the moral development theory that college education is a factor in moral development.

Table 7 - ANALYSIS OF VARIANCE AND MEAN VALUES

Source	Sum of Squares	DF	Mean Squares	F	Significance of F
Main Effects	102.79	1	102.79	2.64	.105
	102.79	1	102.79	2.64	.105
Explained	102.79	1	102.79	2.64	.105
Residual	22640.52	582	38.90		
Total	22743.32	583			

Total Sample Population N = 584
No formal college education, n = 532 X_2 = 44.33
Four or more yrs. of formal college education, n = 52 X_1 = 45.81

ONEWAY Duncan Comparison

The ONEWAY Duncan test was run for categories of employment status, department in the store, and years working with current employer. The results show that managers had a significantly higher PBES mean than those who are working on a part-time basis. There was no significant difference in the PBESs of individuals working in different departments. The ONEWAY Duncan test also shows that individuals who have been working with the host employer between 16-30 years had a significantly higher PBES mean than those who have worked with the host company for less than 16 years.

ONEWAY TEST: Employment Status

Source	D.F.	Sum of Squares	Mean Squares	F Ratio	F Prob.
Between Groups	3	357.8602	119.2867	3.0487	0.0282
Within Groups	598	23398.2544	39.1275		
Total	601	23756.1146			

Mean	Group	1	2	3	4
43.2742	1 - Part-time				
44.0837	2 - Full-time				
44.7820	3 - Assistant Mgr.				
45.4648	4 - Manager		*		

(*) Indicates significant differences at P < .05

General Results of the Hypotheses

The ANOVA results of these hypotheses indicate that age, in general, is a factor in moral development of individuals (see Table 8 for a summary of each hypothesis). The ANOVA results also indicate that supermarket management experience of five or more years is a factor in an individual's moral development. The results further suggest that gender is only a factor in the moral development of those individuals who have no management experience and that females are at a higher level of moral maturity than males. The results also show that ethical views of people are getting much more strict, and that people's ethical expectations are higher than they used to be. The mean PBES for this sample in general is 44.40, which appears to be higher than most previous PBESs completed by Clark's instrument. When comparing current results (Table 8) with previous results (Table 9 in chapter V), it appears that the mean PBES of respondents have increased. The managers with six or more years of experience have higher PBESs than Clark's executives in 1966, and higher than all other studies reviewed in this research. This research further supports the study completed by Stephenson *et al.* in 1995, which concluded that people are much more ethical than they are perceived to be by the general population. The business environment has been perceived to be a "dog-eat-dog" world; however, this study adds a new light to it by concluding that the business world is much more ethical than it is perceived to be.

Table 8 - Summary results of the hypothesis

Hypothesis and Results	Populations	Sample size	St. Dev.	Sample Mean
I - Significant	25 yrs. and younger,	n=121	6.5	42.07
	26 yrs. and older,	n=481	6.10	44.98
II - Not Significant	Males 25 yrs. and younger	n=47	6.23	40.94
	Females 25 yrs. and younger	n=74	6.61	42.78
III - Not Significant	Males 26 yrs. and older	n=263	6.34	44.73
	Females 26 yrs. and older	n=218	5.80	45.29
IV - Significant	More than 5 yrs. of mgmt. exp.	n=165	6.22	45.25
	No mgmt. experience	n=255	6.24	43.62
V - Not Significant	Males > 5yrs. of Mgmt. Exp.	n=146	6.42	45.10
	Females > 5yrs. of Mgmt. Exp.	n=19	4.31	46.42
VI - Significant	Males-no mgmt. Experience	n=65	6.22	41.86
	Females-no mgmt. Experience	n=190	6.15	44.22
VII - Not Significant	No formal college education	n=532	6.23	44.33
	4 or more yrs. of Coll. Education.	n=52	6.32	45.81

The ANOVA results did not find any significant differences between males and females among their age categories. There were no significant differences between males and females with five or more years of supermarket management experience. No significant differences were found between those individuals who had four or more years of college education and those who did not attend college at all.

The ONEWAY Duncan procedure shows that managers had a significantly higher PBES mean than those who are working on a part-time basis. There was no significant difference in the PBESs of individuals working in different departments such as bakery, grocery, market, and deli. The ONEWAY Duncan test also shows that individuals who have been working with the host employer between 16-30 years had a significantly higher PBES mean than those who have worked with the host company for less than 16 years. Overall, it appears that seniority or longevity in the organization seems to be a relevant factor in ethical decision-making. Perhaps future research can test this variable in retail as well as other industries.

Summary
The results were analyzed from the responses of retail employees in the United States. This chapter began with a presentation of demographics of the sample population, reliability analysis, research questions and finally a discussion of the hypotheses. The next chapter summarizes and discusses the findings, provides implication of the findings and the research contributions, mentions the limitations, recommends future research, and ends with a conclusion.

Chapter V contains the implications of this study for the supermarket industry; it compares and integrates the results of this study with previous research.

CHAPTER FIVE

V - CONCLUSIONS

This chapter presents the summary, recommendations and conclusions for this research developed from chapters I – IV. The results of ethics survey and its implications to the supermarket industry are presented in this chapter (V). This chapter compares and contrasts the results with previous studies using Clark's instrument. The study revealed several interesting findings about the relationship of demographic variables and ethical maturity. The following sections present the objectives of the study, research questions and review of related literature, summary of research findings, practical implications, limitations of the study, recommendations for future research, and conclusions.

Introduction

This study concludes that age, management experience, and gender are factors in moral development. The PBES determines one's commitment level of personal integrity and honesty in business dealings and in the observance of the laws governing business. Supermarket associates who are under 26 years of age and have no management experience have significantly lower PBESs than supermarket managers who have six or more years of supermarket management experience. Supermarket associates who are under 26 years of age have significantly lower PBESs than supermarket associates who are at least 26 years of age or older. Male supermarket associates with no management experience have significantly lower PBESs than female supermarket associates with no management experience. One possible explanation might be that males need more responsibility, accountability, awareness of laws and the justice system, and training in order to develop moral maturity, as compared to women. Gilligan (1982) stated that women emphasize sensitivity to others' feelings and rights, and show concern and care for others. While women approach ethical dilemmas from their "care" orientation, men approach ethical dilemmas from a "law and order" orientation, which could suggest that men need to know the facts based on laws, as opposed to their feelings and emotions, to make morally developed decisions.

This study also compared females under 26 years of age with males under 26 years of age, as well as females 26 years of age or older with males who are 26 years of age or older. In both categories, the female population had higher PBES mean; however they were not significantly higher. As mentioned previously, in the sample of males and females who did not have any management experience, the female PBES mean was significantly higher than that of males. This supports Gilligan's research that women are more caring, intimate, helpful, and relationship-oriented, as opposed to men who are more "law and order" oriented. This might be one explanation for the higher PBES mean for females with no management experience. Females with five or more years of supermarket management experience (n=19) have a higher PBES mean than males with five or more years of management experience (n= 146). However, the difference between their scores is not significantly higher (46.42 vs. 45.10). Respondents with four or more years of formal college education (n=52) had a higher PBES mean than those who did not attend college at all (n=532 and 45.81 vs. 44.33). However, these differences were not significant. The sample of respondents with four or more years of college is small compared to those with no college education. A larger sample is needed to confirm or deny this result.

Comparing Results with Previous Research
In general, the PBES means of this study seem to be higher than studies conducted previously using Clark's instrument. This can be seen by comparing the results, PBES mean, of this study from Table 8, chapter IV, with prior results found in table 9 of this chapter. Clark's instrument was created in 1966; and since then many researchers have been using this instrument to evaluate the ethical values of individuals in different industries. Table 9 briefly summarizes the results obtained from those studies using Clark's PBES instrument.

Many of the previous researchers did not use age, management experience, education, or gender as factors. Freedman (1990) was one of the researchers who used age, management experience, and gender as factors affecting moral development. He concluded that age and management experience were positively correlated with the PBESs of the hospitality industry respondents. He further concluded that females had a significantly higher PBES mean than males in the Hospitality Industry. This current study supports Freedman's findings as well as Arrow's research by concluding that age, management experience, and gender are factors in moral development. Peter Arlow (1991) completed a study of 138 business students and concluded that females appear to be more ethical than men. He further concluded that as one matures in age, he or she will put less emphasis on selfish interest versus concern for others. He also stated that the longer the work experience, the lower the concern for selfish interest.

This current study shows that today people are less tolerant of immoral behavior than they were three decades ago in 1966. The managers in this study have a mean PBES of 45.25 and Clark's executives in 1966 had a PBES mean of 43.28. Around 97 percent of Clark's (1966) sample of 103 business executives were in managerial positions - 43 percent were in top management, 38 percent middle management, and 14 percent was composed of the front-line supervisors. Clark's sample were all men; and that may also be an explanation for his sample's lower score because the current sample of 165 managers with six or more years of supermarket management experience includes 19 females whose PBES mean was slightly higher than that of their male counterparts. The PBES mean of individuals who are 25 years of age or younger and have no management experience (42.07) is higher than the PBES mean score of students in the previous studies, as can be seen in table 9, with the exception of Arlow and Ulrich's accounting students who had studied ethics in their auditing class.

Table 9 - Studies using Clark's Instrument

Authors	Year	Sample Populations	Results and Findings
John Clark	1966	Executives	Mean PBES 43.28
Arlow and Ulrich	1980 & 1985	Accounting, Marketing and Management students	Accounting students (42.63)and other majors (39.8)
George Stevens	1984	113 executives and 349 business students	Executives had higher scores (45.52) than students (39.56)
Wynd and Mager	1989	Two yr. study of Business and society students	Business and Society class did not affect PBES scores of students after one semester
Allen Freedman	1990	Hospitality students and managers	Managers with five yrs. of Experience scored higher (41.81) than students (38.73)
Stephenson, Galbraith and Grimm	1995	Five constituent groups of an accredited school	Individuals perceive themselves to be more ethical than others
Mujtaba's study of supermarket associates	1997	Associates and Managers	Managers with five or more yrs. of mgmt. experience scored higher (45.25) than associates w/o mgmt. experience (43.62)

This research was designed to compare the Personal Business Ethics Scores (PBES) of supermarket associates who are under 26 years of age and have no management experience, with the Personal Business Ethics Scores of supermarket managers who are at least 26 years of age and have six or more years of management experience in the supermarket industry. The purpose was to determine whether age and supermarket management experience, gained through the maturation continuum or process, play a role in ethical decision making. This research also ascertained whether education and gender are factors in ethical considerations. The Personal Business Ethics Score consists of eleven scenarios; and measures the respondent's commitment to personal integrity and honesty in the business sector as well as the observance of the laws governing business. The questionnaire was administered to the host supermarket associates and managers in the Central Florida region.

The results of the ANOVA at $P < .05$ indicates that (1) individuals who are under 26 years of age and have no management experience have significantly lower scores than managers with six or more years of supermarket management experience; (2) individuals with six or more years of supermarket management experience have significantly higher scores than those with no management experience; and (3) males with no management experience have significantly lower scores than females with no management experience. There was no significant differences in the PBES of male and female respondents with six or more years of supermarket management experience, as well as those males and females who are under 26 years of age or those who are 26 years of age or older. There was no significant difference in the PBES of respondents with four or more years of formal college education and those who had no formal college education.

This research supports the cognitive moral development theory which states that age, experience, and gender are factors in moral development as stated by Colby, Kohlberg, and Liebert. Individuals under the age of 26 revealed a less ethical stance than those who are at least 26 years of age or older. Also, those with six or more years of management experience have significantly higher scores than those with no management experience. Further, females with no management experience have significantly higher scores than males with no management experience.

There also seems to be a continuum in existence as the score of individuals who are under 26 years of age and have no management experience fall on the low end with a PBES mean of 42.07; next would be the score of females (44.22) with no management experience in the middle of the continuum; and at the highest end would be individuals with six or more years of experience with PBES mean of 45.25. The mean PBES of supermarket associates and managers for this research is higher than previous research using students and managers or executives, with one exception of Steven's (1984) study of executives whose score was slightly higher (45.52 vs. 45.25) than supermarket managers.

Implications for the Supermarket Industry

The results of this survey have some positive implications for the supermarket industry. The results suggest that supermarket management experience, age, and gender make a difference in the moral judgment of individuals. One implication of this research is the role of females in the supermarket industry with regard to gender, specifically that females had a significantly higher PBES mean than males. Since more females are now entering the management sector of the supermarket industry, their higher level of moral maturity could have a positive influence on the level of ethics in this industry in general. Table 10 summarizes the male-female differences in moral reasoning, as described by Leslie Dawson in her 1995 article.

Dawson concludes that women's traits can improve the ethical climate of a firm by bringing more sensitivity, caring treatment of customers, more creative approaches to problem-solving, more effective relationship-building skills, creating greater trust in interpersonal affairs, and being supportive and understanding of supervisory style. She further states that women also can be viewed as less decisive, slower to make decisions, or even naive at times. The best approach might be to combine the best traits of each sex at various levels of management in the organization to have a balance of both sides. This will enable individuals to help each other by effectuating strong solutions to their daily challenges; and they could learn from each other as well.

Table 10 - Male and Female Differences in Moral Reasoning

In solving ethical dilemmas, females are likely to:	In solving ethical dilemmas, males are likely to:
• Primarily respect feelings	• Primarily respect rights
• Ask "who will be hurt?"	• Ask "who is right?"
• Avoid being judgmental	• Value decisiveness
• Search for compromise to achieve fairness	• Make unambiguous decisions based on available data
• Seek solutions that minimize hurt	• Seek solutions that are objectively fair
• Rely on communication	• Rely on rules
• Believe in contextual relativism	• Believe in blind impartiality
• Be guided by emotion	• Be guided by logic
• Challenge authority	• Accept authority

These results also indicate that the host company's emphasis and training on the part of its management may have increased the moral development of its associates. One can only hope that this is true in all companies; and that senior officials are demonstrating, encouraging and enforcing high ethical standards in all their associates, especially their managers.

General Implications and Recommendations
This study has shown that age and management experience are significant factors in the moral development of individuals in the supermarket industry. As individuals grow older and/or gain more management experience, their moral maturity and sophistication grows stronger, and their understanding increases. One possible explanation is that as individuals grow older and gain experience, their understanding of moral issues increases through the daily reinforcement of moral actions in the company or society in general. As Oliver Wendell Holmes said, "Man's mind once stretched by a new idea, never regains its original dimension." Individuals' ability to see beyond the present becomes clear; and their vision of personal integrity and fairness may be the only solution to better living in this interdependent world. Morally sophisticated individuals are also great role models because they know self-mastery is the prerequisite to dealing successfully with others. "I count him braver who overcomes his desires than he who conquers his enemies; for the hardest victory is the victory over self." (Aristotle)

Training and education in ethics also have proven to be a beneficial approach to increase one's moral maturity. This result was concluded from Arlow's and Ulrich's longitudinal study of 1980 and 1985, which showed that Marketing and Management majors scored higher on their post-test as a consequence of completing a Business and Society class that emphasized ethics. Since adults or people who have been in the workforce learn differently than students who are learning in colleges, one should consider diverse adult learning methods, as compared to those for children, and adjust one's strategy and facilitation accordingly.

Pedagogy is the art and science of teaching children. It is derived from the Greek words *paid*, meaning "child", and *agogus*, meaning "leading." The role of the learner is a dependent one. The teacher is expected to determine what is to be learned and how and when it should be learned. Learners are expected to learn the material/content which will be useful at a later date; and their past experience is of no value to the session.

Andragogy is the art and science of teaching adults. It is derived from the Greek words *aner* (with the stem *andr-*) meaning "man, not boy." Great emphasis is placed on the involvement of adult learners in the process of self-diagnosis of the need for learning. As people grow from children to adults, they also move from a dependence stage to more a self-directedness or independence stage; and each individual moves at different dimensions of life differently and at different rates. Finally, they move to an interdependent stage where their success depends on the people around them and not solely on the basis of their own efforts. Andragogy assumes that people will experience greater learning if they see the need for it. They also want their past experiences integrated into the new learning so it makes perfect sense for them. Otherwise, they will not be supportive of the new material.

Following the concepts of Andragogy, it is important that people are taught the universal, timeless, ethical statements, such as the Golden Rule, and the universal principles such as the "law of the harvest," that is, "we reap what we sow." Table 11 lists the Golden Rule, a powerful societal expectation, from different perspectives. The Golden Rule is the universal truth in ethics, though expressed somewhat differently in various cultures and languages; it conveys the same message to everyone regardless of ethnicity or culture. Cultural norms and expectations are very powerful drivers of behavior. Collins (1994), for example, states that creating value and building trust in each relationship with employees, customers and suppliers are instrumental values for ethical and effective management. Ethics can provide value for a firm, including the supermarket industry, if it is being emphasized and reinforced by top management.

Values, however, as well as moral standards, can vary from culture to culture and from time to time; certain values thus can be looked upon as immoral in some cultures by the majority of the population. So, it is important that people are guided by concrete, timeless, universal, objective principles that promote fair practices and justice in the society. Dealing merely with the symptoms of immorality might be analogous to seeing the top of an iceberg and totally ignoring the bottom part which makes up the biggest part of the iceberg. This is similar to the story of Hercules and the seven-headed monster, the Hydra. During their confrontation, as Hercules would cut off one head, two other heads would spring up as its replacement. Finally, he was able to kill the creature after he started cauterizing the stumps of each head, thus totally destroying it. One can see Hydra as the immoral but accepted societal practices and Hercules as the ethical executive who deals with the root of the problem, so it can be totally eliminated. There is a quote by Arnold H. Glasow that says, "The world expects results. Don't tell others about the labor pains-show 'em the baby!", he also says, "The world is not interested in the storms you encountered, but whether you brought in the ship." The moral of these statements would be that solutions worth implementing should eliminate the problem because most often people are interested in the final outcome, a problem-free society, which is what counts in the practical world. So, all solutions should be directly geared toward eliminating the root causes of ethical problems and not just the symptoms.

Table 11 - The Golden Rules

Perspectives	Descriptions	Sources
Brahmanism	This is the sum of duty: Do naught unto other which would cause you pain if done to you.	Mahabharata 5:1517
Buddhism	Hurt not others in ways that you yourself would find hurtful.	Udana-Varga 5:18
Christianity	All things whatsoever ye would that men should do to you, do ye even so to them; for this is the Law and the Prophets.	Matthew 7:12
Confucianism	Surely it is the maxim of loving kindness: Do not unto others what you would not have them do unto you.	Analects 15:23
Islam	No one of you is a believer until he desires for his brother that which he desires for himself.	Quran-The Teachings of Islam
Judaism	What is hateful to you, do not to your fellowman. That is the entire Law; all the rest is commentary.	Talmud, Shabbat 31a
Taoism	Regard your neighbor's gain as your own gain and your neighbor's loss as your own losses.	T'ai Shang Kan Ying P'ien
Zoroastrianism	That nature alone is good which refrains from doing unto another whatsoever is not good for itself.	Dadistan-i-dinik 94:5

Aristotle said it first over thousands of years ago, and the same principle and concept still holds true today:

You get a good adult by habituating a good child to doing the right thing. Praise for truth-telling and sanctions for fibbing well, in time, make him *or her* "naturally" honest. Abstract knowledge of right and wrong no more contributes to character than knowledge of physics contributes to cycling (Michael Levine, NY Times, 1989).

The same habitual approach applies to adults as well as children, because learning and moral development does not stop at adolescence but continue throughout one's life. Formal as well as informal education and training in ethics, therefore, are critical in the business sector; and can make a difference in creating an awareness of sensitive ethical dilemmas and solutions which lead to and reflect moral behavior. Arlow and Ulrich (1980) found that management and marketing students had significantly lower PBESs than the accounting students. They attributed the accountant students' higher score to the students' having taken an auditing class in which they had studied professional ethics. They further stated that the management and marketing students did not have any exposure to professional ethics in any of their courses.

All education and training should be geared to encourage moral behavior and conduct. Thomas Carlisle stated that "Conviction is worthless unless it is converted into conduct." There are many formats in which ethics training can be delivered to the associates of an organization. Some common ethics training sessions are being delivered through seminars, lectures, role-playing exercises, multimedia training or case studies, memos, and employee codes of conduct programs. This training should be delivered by ethicists or professional facilitators who are familiar with the firm's prospective ethical issues and challenges. In order to promote high ethical standards and reduce or even eliminate unfair practices in any business or industry, executives and managers should at least receive training and education in the following areas:

1. Individuals should receive training and instructions in the systems of justice and equity based on their corporate culture, legal systems, and society. They should be made aware of the prevailing laws, regulations, and practices that govern their conduct. They should also be encouraged to go above and beyond the laws to make decisions that are moral and positively affect the lives of other people.

2. They should be made well aware of their own and their associates' legal and ethical rights, obligations, expectations, and responsibilities. These expectations and responsibilities need to be clearly communicated to all the firm's stakeholders.

3. Executives and managers should be continuously reminded of the standards of objectivity, fairness, integrity, and maturity, as well as the need to have consideration for others and the courage to stand for what they believe is right. They should be taught persistently high standards of legal and moral behavior, which embody integrity, self-respect, justice, and fairness in their relationships with everyone, personally and professionally. They must be the role models in the organization; and accordingly they must behave exactly in the manner that they would want their finest associates to behave. As Dwight Lyman Moody said, "If I take care of my character, my reputation will take care of itself." If each individual in the company acts with honesty and integrity, then the company's reputation will take of itself.

4. Executives and managers should be guided, and supported in making decisions that emphasize responsiveness and accountability to the truth because "the truth will, eventually, set you free." They should also be instructed to avoid using

their position and title to perpetuate sole self-interest or mere private gain. Honesty to oneself is the best policy and "those who know the truth are not equal to those who love it, and those who love it are not equal to those who live it" (Confucius). Thus, they should legally and morally promote value, not only for themselves, but also for their firms, its stakeholders, and society in general.

Limitations and Future Research
The findings and limitations of this study provide several avenues for future research. This study used a relatively small sample from a single company and from a single site in the Florida area. Characteristics unique to the host company (e.g., organizational policies and political circumstances) may have influenced the findings of this research. This study used associates from only one supermarket, so the results of this study do not represent the ethical values of all supermarket employees and managers in the United States, or even in Florida. Future research studies can survey employees of several retail outlets in different regions and locations across the United States to see if their results are similar to or different from these findings. Perhaps organizational culture, training on ethics, size of the firm, and number of employees can be part of the research factors.

This research compared the ethical responses of supermarket associates who are 25 years of age or younger and have no management experience, with managers who are 26 years of age or older and have at least six or more years of supermarket management experience. Within the associate and management populations, there are people from different cultures, with and without management experience, who are under the age of 26 and over the age of 26. Further research using the Clark instrument could compare the responses of these populations based on their ethnic backgrounds to see if age, management experience, gender, and education are factors in their moral development. This would tell us if ethnicity plays a factor in moral development of individuals, based on their age, management experience, education, and gender.

The working environment is changing rapidly. Women, Asians, Native Americans, older individuals, immigrants from many nations, Blacks, Hispanics, and differently-abled individuals are beginning to replace the traditional "white male" as the largest segment of the workforce. Therefore, it would be very helpful, and quite interesting, to determine if ethnicity plays a factor in the ethical decision-making process.

Conclusions
The moral development theory is sustained by this research. Age, management experience, and gender are factors which affect the moral development of supermarket associates and managers, as shown by their evaluation of, and solution to business dilemmas. Gilligan stated that females have higher moral values than males; and this research supports her statement.

All individuals are responsible for deepening their understanding of "right" and "wrong" conduct as they grow older. This study shows that age is a factor in the moral development of individuals; and each person has the capacity to become morally sophisticated as he or she gets older and becomes mature. This study concludes that age and management experience are both factors in moral maturity.

Since people are the common denominator of success and effectiveness, attaining progress and improvement are impossible ends with ineffective or un-improvable people as means. The best way to promote fairness and cooperation, and to improve and empower people, is to educate and liberate them so they can take proper responsibility for their own choices in life, whether personal, professional, or business. One must become effective individually (privately and personally) before one can be effective with others, which is very important in this interdependent world. One must learn, not only how to create value for oneself, but also for others; and to do so in a legal, ethical, and socially responsible manner.

REFERENCES

VI - Bibliography

Alexander, M. A. (2004). Job satisfaction and organizational commitment in the local church: A study of African American male ministers (Doctoral dissertation, Nova Southeastern University). *Dissertation Abstracts International, 65 (01)*. (UMI No.3119761).

Alkadry, M. G., & Tower, L.E. (2006). Unequal pay: The role of gender. *Public Administration Review, 66 (6)*, 888 – 898.

Abratt, R., Nel, D., & Higgs, N.S. (1992). An Examination of the Ethical Beliefs of Managers Using Selected Scenarios in a Cross-Cultural Environment. *Journal of Business Ethics*, 11, 29-35.

Adeyemi-Bello, T. (1994). Work Values of Males and Females: A Developing Country's Example. International Journal of Management, 11(4), 940-945.

Andrews, K. R. (1989, Sept-Oct). Ethics in practice, *Harvard Business Review*, pp. 99-104.

Arlow, P. (1991). Personal Characteristics in College Students' Evaluations of Business Ethics and Corporate Social Responsibility. *Journal of Business Ethics*, 10, 63-69.

Arlow, P., & Ulrich, T.A. (1980). Business ethics, social responsibility and business students: An empirical comparison of Clark's study. *Akron Business and Economic Review*, pp. 17-22.

Arlow, P., & Ulrich, T. A. (1985). Business ethics and business school graduates: A longitudinal study. *Akron Business Review*, 13-17.

Arlow, P., & Ulrich, T. A. (1988). A longitudinal survey of business school graduates' assessments of business ethics. *Journal of Business Ethics*, 7, 295-302.

Arnst, C. (1996, January 15). The bloodletting at AT&T is just the beginning. *Business Week*, p. 30.

Badenhorst, J.A. (1994). Unethical behavior in procurement: A perspective on causes and solutions. *Journal of Business Ethics*, 13, 739-745.

Baumhart, S. J. (1961). How ethical are business-men? *Harvard Business Review*, 39. pp. 6-9.

Babbie, E. (1992). The practice of social research (6th ed.). Wadsworth Publishing Company.

Baxter, D. G., & Rarick, A. C. (1987). Education for the moral development of managers: Kohlberg's stages of moral development and integrative education. *Journal of Business Ethics*, 6, 243-248.

Beauchamp, T. L. (1988). Ethical theory and its application to business. In T. L. Beauchamp, & N. E. Bowie (Eds.), Ethical Theory and Business (3rd ed.) (pp. 1-55). Prentice Hall: Englewood Cliffs.

Becker, H., & Fritsche, D. (1987). Business ethics: A cross-cultural comparison of managers' attitudes. *Journal of Business Ethics*, 6, 289-295.

Beltramini, R. F. (1984). Concerns of college students regarding business ethics. *Journal of Business Ethics*, 3, 195-200.

Bishop, T. R. (1992). Integrating business ethics into an undergraduate curriculum. *Journal of Business Ethics*, 11, 291-299.

Brenner, S. N. (1992). Ethics programs and their dimensions. Journal of Business Ethics, 11, 391-9.

Brenner, S. N., & Molander, E. A. (1977). Is the ethics of business changing? *Harvard Business Review*, 55, 57-71.

Bromiley, P., & Marcus, A. (1989). The deterrent to dubious corporate behavior: Profitability, probability and safety recalls. *Strategic Management Journal*, 10, 251-271.

Brown, M. K. (1994). Using role play to integrate ethics into the business curriculum: A financial management example. *Journal of Business Ethics*, 13, 105-111.

Carr, A. Z. (1994). Is business bluffing ethical?. In J. Drummond & B. Bain (Eds.), Managing business ethics (pp. 26-38). Butterworth-Heinemann Ltd.

Carmichael, S., & Drummond, J. (1989). Good business (1st ed.). Published in London.

Carroll, A. B. (1975). Managerial ethics: A post-Watergate view. *Business Horizons*, 2, 75-80.

Cava, A. (1990). Teaching ethics: A moral model. *Business and Economics Review*, 36(3), 10-13.

Cavanagh, F. G. (1990). American business values. Englewood Cliffs, New Jersey: Prentice Hall.

Cavanagh, F. G., Moberg, J. D., & Velasquez, M. (1995). Making business ethics practical. *Business Ethics Quarterly*. pp. 398 - 418.

Cavico, F. J. (1993). Invasion of privacy in the private employment sector: Tortious and ethical aspects. *Houston Law Review*, 30(3).

Center for Business Ethics. (1986). Are corporations institutionalizing ethics? *Journal of Business Ethics*, 5, 85-91.

Chap, J. (1985). Moral judgment in middle and late adulthood: The effects of age appropriate moral dilemmas and spontaneous role taking. *International Journal of Aging and Human Development*, 22, 161-171.

Clark, J. W., & Clark, S.J. (1966). Religion and moral standards of American businessmen. Cincinnati: Southwestern Publishing Co.

Clarkson, Max B. E. (1995). A stakeholder framework for analyzing and evaluating corporate social performance. *Academy of Management Review*, 20.

Cohen, J., Pant L., & Sharp D. (1993). A validation and extension of a multidimensional ethics scale. *Journal of Business Ethics*, 12, 13-26.

Colby, A., & Damon W. (1992). Some do care: Contemporary lives of moral commitment. The Free Press. Review By Lisa Kuhmerker in Moral Education Forum.

Colby, A., Damon, W., & Kohlberg, L. (1984). Invariant sequence and internal consistency in moral judgment stages. In W. M. Kurtines & J.L. Gewirtz (eds.). Morality, moral behavior, and development (pp. 41-52). New York: John Wiley and Sons.

Collins, W. J. (1994, September/October). Is business ethics an oxymoron? *Business Horizons*, pp. 1-8.

Cooke, R. A. (1986). Business ethics at a crossroad. *Journal of Business Ethics*, 5, 259-263.

Covey, R. S. (1990). The 7 habits of highly effective people: Powerful Lessons in Personal Change. New York: First Fireside Edition.

Cox, A.D., Cox, D., Anderson, R.D., & Moschis, G.P. (1993). Social influences on adolescent shoplifting-theory, evidence, and implications for the retail industry. *Journal of Retailing*, 69(2), 234-246.

Crittenden, P. (1990). Learning to be moral: Philosophical thoughts about moral development. New Jersey: Humanities Press International, Inc.

Cullen, J. B., B. Victor, & C. Stephens (1989). An ethical weather report: Assessing the organizational climate. *Organizational dynamics*, pp. 50-62.

Davis, P. (1995). Are your employees legal? *Business Ethics*, 9(6), 22-23.

Dawson, M. L. (1995, July/August). Women and men, morality and ethics. *Business Horizons*, 38.

Davis, J. (1994). Good ethics is good for business: Ethical attributions and response to environmental advertising. *Journal of Business Ethics*, 13, 873-885.

Dean, J. P. (1992). Making codes of ethics "Real". *Journal of Business Ethics*, 11, 285-290.

DeGeorge, R. T. (1995). Business ethics (4th ed.). New Jersey: Prentice Hall Inc.

DeGeorge, R. T. (1989). Business ethics (2nd. ed.) (pp. 1-44). New York: Macmillan.

DeGeorge, R. T. (1987). The status of business ethics: Past present and future. Journal of Business Ethics, 6, 202-211.

Delany, J. T., & Sockell, D. (1992). Do company ethics training programs make a difference? An empirical analysis. *Journal of Business Ethics*, 11, 719-727.

Deemer, K. D., & College, A. (1992). Moral judgment and life experience. *Moral education forum*, pp. 11-22.

Dieterly, D., & Schneider, B. (1974). The effect of organizational environment on perceived power and climate: A laboratory study. *Organizational Behavior and Human Performance*, 11, 316-337.

Dobson, J. (1993, November-December). The role of ethics in finance. *Financial Analyst Journal*, 57-62.

Donaldson, J., & Davis, P. (1990). Business ethics? Yes, but what can it do for the bottom line. *Management Decisions*, 28, 29-33.

Donaldson, T., & Preston, L. E. (1995). The stakeholder theory of the corporation: Concepts, evidence, and implications. *Academy of Management Review*, 20(1).

Drucker, F. P. (1994). What is "Business Ethics"?. In Wines, A. W. and Stevens, A. Reading in business ethics and social responsibility (pp. 54-59). Iowa: Kendall and Hunt Publishing.

Drummond, J., & Bain, B. (1994). Managing business ethics. Butterworth-Heinemann Ltd.

Dubinsky, A. J. (1983). Identifying and addressing retail salespeople's ethical problems: A method and application. *Journal of Retailing*, 59(1), 46-66.

Elias, M. (1996, January 10). Fatty diet, lead levels in blood linked. USA Today,(D).

Falkenberg, L., & Herremans, I. (1995). Ethical behaviors in organizations: Directed by the formal or Informal systems? *Journal of Business Ethics*, 14, 133-143.

Field, R. H. G., & Abelson, M. A. (1982). Climate: A reconceptualization and proposed model. *Human Relations*, 5, 181-201.

Fisher, D. H., & Fowler, S.B. (1995). Re-imaging moral leadership in business: Image, identity and difference. *Business Ethics Quarterly*, 5(1).

Fleishman, E. A. (1953). Leadership climate, human relations training, and supervisory behavior. *Personnel Psychology*, pp. 205-222.

Ford, R. C., & Richardson, W.D. (1994). Ethical decision making: A review of the empirical Literature. *Journal of Business Ethics*, 205-221.

Freedman, A. (1990). Business ethics survey of hospitality students and managers. DBA Dissertation at Nova Southeastern University.

Freeman, R., & Gilbert, D. (1988). Corporate strategy and the search for ethics. Englewood Cliffs, NJ: Prentice-Hall.

Friedman, M. (1994). The social responsibility of business is to increase its profits. In A. W. Wines and A. Stevens (Eds.), Reading in business ethics and social responsibility (pp. 137-141). Iowa: Kendall and Hunt Publishing.

Fritzche, D. J. (1995). Personal values: Potential keys to ethical decision making. *Journal of Business Ethics* 14, 909-922.

Gellerman, S. W. (1986). Why 'good' managers make bad ethical decisions. *Harvard Business Review*, 64, 85-91.

Ghoshal, S. (2005). Bad management theories are destroying good management practices. *Academy of Management Learning and Education*, (4(1), 75-91.

Gilligan, C. (1982). In a difference voice: Psychological theory and women's development. Cambridge, MA: Harvard University Press.

Gilligan, C. (1977). In a different voice: Women's conception of self and morality. *Harvard Educational Review*, 47, 481-517.

Glenn, R. J., Jr. (1992). Can a business and society course affect the ethical judgment of future managers? *Journal of Business Ethics*, 11, 217-223.

Glenn, R. J., Jr. (1990). Business students ethics: Implications for professors and managers. In C. Walton (Ed.), Enriching business ethics (pp. 213-231). New York and London: Plenum Press.

Glick, W. (1985). Conceptualizing and measuring organizational and psychological climate: Pitfalls in multi-level research. *Academy of Management Review*, 11, 601-616.

Goodstein, R. C. (1994). UPC scanner pricing systems: Are they accurate? *Journal of Marketing,* 58.

Graham, J. W. (1995). Leadership, moral development and citizenship behavior. *Business Ethics Quarterly,* 5(1), 43-54.

Hallaq, H. J., & Steinhorst, K. (1994). Business intelligence methods-how ethical. *Journal of Business Ethics,* 13, 787-794.

Handy, C. (1996). Beyond certainty: The changing worlds of organizations. Harvard Business School Press.

Harris, J. R. (1990). Ethical values of individuals at different levels in the organizational hierarchy of a single firm. *Journal of Business Ethics,* 9, 741-750.

Harris, J. R., & Sutton, D. C. (1995). Unravelling the ethical decision-making process: Clues from an empirical study comparing Fortune 1000 executives and MBA students. *Journal of Business Ethics,* 14.

Havighurst, R. J. (1994). Developmental tasks. In J. M. Rich & L. J. DeVitis (eds.), Theories of moral development (2nd. ed) (pp. 50-54). Charles Thomas Publishing.

Hegarty, W. H., & Sims, H. P., Jr. (1978). Some determinants of unethical decision behavior: An experiment. *Journal of Applied Psychology,* 63, 451-457.

Hegarty, W. H., & Sims, H. P., Jr. (1979). Organizational philosophy, policies, and objectives related to unethical decision behavior: A laboratory experiment. *Journal of Applied Psychology,* 64, 331-338.

Hemming, J. (1991). The physiology of moral maturity. Journal of Moral Education, 20(2), 127-138.

Hochstein, M. (1985). Tax ethics: Social values and noncompliance. *Social Issues Resources Series,* 2, Article #64.

Hoffman, W.M. (1994). What is necessary for corporate moral excellence? In J. Drummond & B. Bain (ed.), Managing business ethics, Butterworth-Heinemann Ltd.

Honeycutt, E. D., Siguaw, J.A., & Hunt, T.G. (1995). Business ethics and job-related constructs: A cross-cultural comparison of automotive salespeople. *Journal of Business Ethics,* 14, 235-248.

Hosmer, T. L. (1994). Moral leadership in business. Homewood,IL: Richard D. Irwin, Homewood.

Hosmer, T. L. (1994). Strategic planning as if ethics mattered. *Strategic Management Journal,* 15, 17-34, 17-35.

Howell, J. M., & Avolio, B. J. (1992). The ethics of charismatic leadership: Submission or liberation?. *Academy of Management Review,* 6(2).

Izraeli, D. (1988). Ethical beliefs and behavior of managers: A cross-cultural perspective. *Journal of Business Ethics,* 7, 263-271.

Jadack, R. A., Hyde, J. S., Moore, C. F., & Keller, M. L. (1995). Moral reasoning about sexually transmitted diseases. *Child Development,* 66, 167-177.

Jensen, M. C., & Meckling, W. H. (1976, October). Theory of the firm: Managerial behavior, agency costs and ownership structure. *Journal of Financial Economics,* 305-360.

Jones, P. (1993). Productivity Seminar. Nova Southeastern University. Ft. Lauderdale, Florida.

Kaltenheuser, S. (1995, May/June). Doing business under an immoral government china. *Business Ethics,* Vol. 9, 9(3), 20-24.

Kavathatzopoulos, I. (1991). Kohlberg and Piaget: Differences and similarities. *Journal of Moral Education*, 20(1), 47-54.

Kerlinger, F. N. (1986). Foundation of behavioral research, 3rd. ed. CBS College Publishing: New York.

Keller, M., & Edelstein, W. (1993, April). The development of a moral self from childhood to adolescence. *Moral Education Forum*, pp. 1-18.

Kidwell, J. M., Steven, R. E., & Bethke, A. L. (1987). Differences in ethical perceptions between male and female managers: Myth or reality? *Journal of Business Ethics*, pp. 489-493.

Kochunny, C. M., & Rogers, H. (1994). Head-heart disparity among future managers: Implications for ethical conduct. *Journal of Business Ethics*, 13, 719-729.

Kohlberg, L. (1984). The Philosophy of Moral Development, San Francisco: Harper and Row.

Kohlberg, L. (1972). A cognitive-developmental approach to moral education. *The Humanist*, 4, 13-16.

Kohlberg, L. (1969). Stage and sequence: The cognitive- developmental approach to socialization. In D. Grosling (ed.), Handbook of socialization theory and research, Chicago: Rand McNally.

Kotter, J., & Heskett, J. (1992). Corporate culture and performance. New York: Free Press.

Kuper, L. (1975). Race, science and society. The Unescor Press and Columbia University Press.

Kurtines, M. W., & Gewirtz. (1984). Morality, moral behavior, and moral development. New York: John Wiley and Sons.

Kurtines, M. W., & Gewirtz. (1987). Moral development through social interaction. New York: John Wiley and Sons.

Lee, R. D., & McKenzie, B. R. (1995, Winter). How the marketplace fosters business honesty. *Business and Society Review*, 92.

Lee, K. H., Tse, K. D., Vertinsky, I., & Wehrung, A.D. (1994). Responsible business behavior: A comparison of managers' perceptions in the People's Republic of China, Hong Kong, and Canada. In M. Hoffman, J. Damm, R. Frederick, & E. Petry, Jr. (Eds.), Emerging global business ethics. Quorum Books

Levine, Michael (1989). "Can ethics be taught?". New York Times, *New York Times Inc.*, November 25, 1989, 4.

Lichtenstein, M. B., Beverly, A. S., & Torbert, R. W. (1995). Leadership and ethical development: Balancing light and shadow. *Business Ethics Quarterly*, 5(1), 97-116.

Liebert, R. M. (1984). What develops in moral development?. In W.M. Kurtines & J.L. Gewirtz (eds), Morality, moral behavior, and development (pp. 177-192). New York: John Wiley and Sons.

Litwin, G. H., & Stringer, R. A. (1968). Motivation and organizational climate. Harvard Business Review. Division of Research, Boston.

Livingston, S. J. (1988, September-October). Pygmalion in management. *Harvard Business Review,* pp. 121-131.

Martin, Petty, Keown, & Scott. (1991). Basic financial management (5th ed). Prentice-Hall, Inc..

Mason, M. G., & Gibbs, J. C. (1993, October). Role-taking opportunities and the transition to advanced moral Judgment. *Moral Education Forum,* pp. 1-13.

McDonald, M. G., & Donleavy, D. G. (1995). Objections to the teaching of business ethics. *Journal of Business Ethics,* 14, 839-853.

McDonald, G., & Zepp, R. (1994). Business ethics: practical proposals. In J. Drummond & B. Bain (eds.). Managing business ethics. Butterworth-Heinemann Ltd.

Mitroff, I. I. (2004). An open letter to the deans and faculties of American business schools. *Journal of Business Ethics,* 54, pp. 185-189.

Moremont, M. (1995, October). Blind ambition. Business Week. pp. 78-80.

Moody, R. H. (1994). Moral development over the life-span. *Moral Education Forum,* pp. 2-16.

Moore, J. (1990). What is really unethical about insider trading? *Journal of Business Ethics,* 9, 171-182.

Morris, C. G. (1982). Psychology: An introduction (4th ed.). New Jersey: Prentic-Hall, Inc.

Moser, M. R. (1988). Ethical conflict at work: A critique of the literature and for future research. *Journal of Business Ethics,* 7, 381-387.

Mujtaba, B. G. (1996). Ethics and morality in business. *Journal of Global Competitiveness,* Vol. 4 (1), PP. 339 - 346.

Murphy, R. P., Smith, E. J., & Daley, M. J. (1992). Executive attitude, organizational size and ethical issues: Perspectives on a service industry. *Journal of Business Ethics,* 11, 11-19.

Nagy, R. A., & Obenberger, R. W. (1994, July-August). Factors   influencing individual investor behavior. *Financial Analyst Journal,* 63-71.

Nash, L. L. (1994). Why business ethics now?. In J. Drummond & B. Bain. Managing business ethics (pp. 7-25). Butterworth-Heinemann Ltd.

Neubaum, D. O., Pagell, M., Drexler Jr., J. A., McKee-Ryan, F. M., and Larson, E. (2009). Business Education and Its Relationship to Student Personal Moral Philosophies and Attitudes Toward Profits: An Empirical Response to Critics. *Academy of Management Learning and Education,* 8(1), pp. 9-24.

Nicholson, N. (1994). Ethics in organizations: A framework for theory and research. *Journal of Business Ethics,* 13, 581-596.

Ostapski, S. A., & Isaacs, N. C. (1992). Corporate moral responsibility and the moral audit: Challenges for Refuse Relief Inc. *Journal of Business Ethics,* 11, 231-239.

Paradise, L. V. (1977). Toward a theory on the ethical behavior of counselors. Dissertation Abstracts International, 37, 4140A-4141A.

Peek, R., & Havighurst, R. (1962). The psychology of character development. New York: John Wiley and Sons.

Perrow, C. (1961). The analysis of goals in complex organizations. *American Sociological Review,* 26, 854-866.

Piaget, J. (1975). The moral judgment of the child. In H. Brown & R. Stevens (Eds), Social behavior and experience, (pp. 221-236). England: Open University.

Philips, M. (1984). Bribery and ethics (2nd ed.). Chicago, pp. 280-290.

Philips, M. (1995). Corporate moral responsibility: When it might matter. *Business Ethics Quarterly,* pp. 555-574.

Posner, B. Z., Kouzes, M., & Schmidt, W. H. (1985). Shared values make a difference: An empirical test of corporate culture. *Human Resource Management*, 24(3), 293-309.

Posner, B. A., Kouzes, M., & Schmidt, W. H. (1987). Ethics in America: A managerial perspective. *Journal of Business Ethics*, 6, 383-391.

Pratt W.M.,Golding G., Hunter W. (1988). "From Inquiry to Judgment: Age and Sex Differences in Patterns of Adult Moral Thinking and Information-Seeking", International *Journal of Aging and Human Development,* Volume 27(2), Pages 109 - 124.

Quinn, P. D., & Jones, M. T. (1995). An agent morality of business policy. *Academy of Management Review,* 20(1), 22-42.

Rest, R. J., & Narvaez, D. (1994). Moral development in the profession: Psychology and applied ethics. Hillsadale, N.J.: Lawrence Erlbaum Associates, Review by Lisa Kuhmerker, Moral Education Forum.

Rest, R. J. (1986). Moral development: Advances in research and theory. New York: Praeger.

Rest, R. J., & Thoma, S. J. (1985). Relation of moral judgment development to formal education. *Developmental Psychology*, 21, 709-714.

Reidenbach, R. E., & Robin, D. P. (1995). A Response to "On Measuring Ethical Judgments." *Journal of Business Ethics* 14, 159-162.

Rice, P. F. (1995). Human development: A life-span approach (2nd ed.). New Jersey: Prentice Hall.

Rich, J. M., & DeVitis, L. J. (1994). Theories of moral development (2nd ed.). Charles Thomas Publishing.

Richter, A., & Barnum, C. (1994, September). When values clash. *HR Magazine*, pp. 42-45.

Ries, I. S. (1992). An intervention curriculum for moral development. *Journal of Moral Education,* 21(1), 41-58.

Rogers, B. (1994, September). Serious about its code of ethics. *HR Magazine*, pp. 46-48.

Ruegger, D., & King, E. W. (1992). A study of the effects of age and gender upon students business ethics. *Journal of Business Ethics*, 11, 179-186.

Savickas, R. J. (1995, November/December). The business of ethics. HR Echoes. SHRM Newsletter.

Schaupp, L. D., & Lane, S. M. (1992). Teaching business ethics: Bringing reality to the classroom. *Journal of Business Ethics*, 11, 225-229.

Schneider, B. (1975). Organizational climate: An essay. *Personnel Psychology*, 28, 447-479.

Schneider, B., & Reichers, A. E. (1983). On the etiology of climates. *Personal Psychology*, 36, 19-36.

Schonert-Reichl, K. A. (1995). Peer relationship, social behavior, and the development of moral reasoning during pre- and early adolescence. *Moral Education Forum,* pp. 21-33.

Schroeder, M. (1996, February 12). Stinging small business. Business Week, pp. 54-60.

Servinek, P. J. (1992). Demographic and related differences in ethical views among small businesses. *Journal of Business Ethics,* 11, 555-566.

Shaw, H. W., & Barry, V. (1992). Moral issues in business (5th ed.). Wadsworth Publishing.

Shea, F. G. (1988). Practical ethics. AMA Publications.

Shefrin, H., & Statman, M. (1993, November-December). Ethics, fairness and efficiency in financial markets. *Financial Analysts Journal,* 21-29.

Shepard, J. M., Shepard, J., Wimbush, J. C., & Stephens, C. U. (1995). The place of ethics in business: Shifting paradigms? *Business Ethics Quarterly,* pp. 577-601.

Shine, R. (1994, November-December). Ethics training for accountants. Written by David W. Farrell & Novella N. Clevenger. New accountants, pp. 22-26.

Sikula, A., Sr. and Costa, D. A. (1994). Are women more ethical than men? *Journal of Business Ethics,* 13, 859-871.

Sims, R. R. (1994). Ethics and organizational decision making: A call for renewal. London: Quorum Books.

Sims, R. R. (1992). The challenge of ethical behavior in organization. *Journal of Business Ethics,* 11, 505-513.

Sims, R. R., & Sims, J. J. (1991). Increasing applied business ethics in business school curricula. *Journal of Business Ethics,* 10, 211-220.

Smith, T. S., McGuire, J. M., Abbott, D. W., & Blau, B. I. (1991). Clinical ethical decision making: An investigation of the rationales used to justify doing less than one believes one should. *Professional Psychology: Research and Practice,* 22, 235-239.

Solberg, J., Strong, C. K., & McGuire, C., Jr. (1995). Living (not learning) ethics. *Journal of Business Ethics,* 14, 71-81.

Solomon, R. C. (1994). New world of business: Ethics and free enterprise in the global 1991's (2nd ed.) (pp. 33-78). Published by Rowman and Littlefield Publishers, Inc.

Stephenson, H. B., Galbraith, S., & Grimm, R. B. (1995). Ethical congruency of constituent groups. *Journal of Business Ethics,* 14, 145-158.

Stevens, G. F. (1984). Business ethics and social responsibility: The response of present and future managers. *Akron Business and Economic Review,* pp. 6-11.

Stoner, J. F., & Freeman, R. E. (1989). Management (4th ed.). New Jersey: Prentice Hall.

Sutton, B. (1993). The legitimate corporations: Essential readings in business ethics and corporate governance (pp. 105-178). Basil Blackwell Ltd. Publishers.

Takala, T., & Uusitalo, O. (1995). Retailers' professional and profession-ethical dilemmas: The case of Finnish retailing business. *Journal of Business Ethics,* 14, 893-907.

Torbert, W. (1991). The power of balance: Transforming self, society, and scientific inquiry. Newbury Park, California: Sage.

Tsalikis, J., & Nwachukwu, O. (1988). Cross-cultural business ethics: Ethical beliefs. Difference between black and white. *Journal of Business Ethics*, 7, 745-754.

Tsalikis, J., & Nwachukwu, O. (1989). Cross-cultural marketing ethics: An investigation on the ethical beliefs & differences between Greeks and Americans. *Journal of International Consumer Marketing*, 1, 3-15.

Trudeau, K. (1992). Mega memory. American Memory Institute. Audio tapes and Workshop.

Velasquez, M. G. (1988). Why corporations are not morally responsible for anything they do. In T. L Beauchamp & N. E. Bowie (Eds.), Ethical theory and Business (3rd ed.) (pp. 69-76). Prentice Hall.

Victor, B., & Cullen, J.B. (1987). A theory and measure of ethical climate in organizations. *Research in Corporate Social Performance and Policy*, 9, 57-71.

Vitell, S. J., & Festervand, F. A. (1987). Business ethics: Conflict, practice, and beliefs of industrial executives. *Journal of Business Ethics*, 6, 111-122.

Walker, L. (1986). Experiential and cognitive sources of moral development in adulthood. *Human Development*, 29, 113-124.

Walker, L. (1995, February). Whither moral psychology? *Moral Education Forum*, pp. 1-8.

Wallace, D. (1995, July/August). Cooking the books: What would you do? *Business Ethics*, 9(4).

Walton, C. C. (1990). Enriching business ethics (pp. 213-231). New York and London: Plenum Press.

Western, K. (1995). Ethical spying. Business Ethics, 9(5), 22-23.

White, L. P., & Rhodenback, M. J. (1992). Ethical dilemmas in organization development: A cross-cultural analysis. *Journal of Business Ethics*, 11, 663-670.

Wimbush, C. James and Shepard, M. Jon (1994). "Toward An Understanding of Ethical Climate: Its Relationship to Ethical Behavior and Supervisory Influence", *Journal of Business Ethics,* 13, Pages 637 - 647.

White, B. C. (1988). Age, education, and sex effects on adult moral reasoning. *International Journal of Aging and Human Development*, 27(4), 271-281.

Wines, A. W., & Stevens, A. (1994). Reading in business ethics and social responsibility. Iowa: Kendall and Hunt Publishing.

Winkle, G. N. (1995). The growth of moral motivation. *Moral Education Forum*, pp. 8-20.

Wise, D.A. (1975). Academic achievement and job performance. *The American Economic Review, 65 (3)*, 350-366.

Wolfe, A. (1993, May-June). We've had enough business ethics. *Business Horizons*, pp. 1-3.

Wood, D. (1990). Business and society (pp. 194-229). Published in United States.

Wood, J. (2006). Opportunity, ease, encouragement, and shame: A short course in pitching for-profit education. *The Chronicle of Higher Education, 52 (19)*, B10.

Wynd, W. R., & Mager, J. (1989). The business and society course: Does it change student attitudes? Journal of Business Ethics, 8(6), 486-491.

Young, I. P. (1997). Dimensions of employee compensation: Practical and theoretical implications for superintendents. *Educational Administration Quarterly, 33,* 506-525.

VII - APPENDIX

Business Ethics Survey
This study is primarily concerned with the Business Ethics view of managers and non-managers. You are not required to record your name and the information you provide will be totally confidential. Please check the appropriate sections; and your cooperation deserves my heart-felt thanks and gratitude.

A.   What is your gender?   1.____Male   2.____Female

B.   What is your age?
          1.____16 - 25   2.____26 - 35 3.____36 -45
          4.____46 - 55   5.____56 or above

C.   How would you describe yourself?
          1____White, not of Hispanic origin
          2____Black, not of Hispanic origin
          3____Hispanic   4____Asian/Pacific Islander
          5____American Indian/Alaskan Native
          6____Other (please specify) _____

D.   Were you born in the United States?
          1.____Yes (Skip the next question)   2.____No

E.   If you answered No to D, how many years have you lived in the U.S.?
          1.___Less than one year 2.___1 - 5 years
          3.___6 - 10 years   4.___11 - 19 years
          5.___20 or more years

F.   What is the highest academic schooling you have acquired?
          1.___Less than twelve years
          2.___High School Diploma or Equivalent
          3.___Two years of College or Institute Training
          4.___Bachelors Degree   5.___Masters Degree
          6.___Doctorate Degree
          7.___Other (please specify)_____

G.   How long have you worked with your current employer?
          1.___Less than one year 2.___1 - 5 years 3.___6 - 15 years
          4.___16 -30 yrs.
          5.___30 or more years

H.   Have you ever worked in a management position?
        1.___Yes   2.___No (skip the next two questions)

I.   How many years of Management experience do you have regardless of
        industry?
        1.___ less than one year   2.___1-5 years   3.___6-10 years
        4.___11-15 years   5.___16 or more years

J.   How many years have you worked in various management positions in the
        Supermarket industry?
        1.___less than one year   2.___1-5 years   3.___6-10 years
        4.___11-15 years   5.___16 or more years

K.   Are you currently:
        1.___Part-time   2.___Full-time (non-management)
        3.___Asst. Manager   4.___Manager

L.   Which is your current department?
        1.___Grocery\Store   2.___Meat   3.___Produce\Floral
        4.___Bakery   5.___Deli

Please circle the answer which best expresses your judgment of each case.

1. *A number of high-ranking executives of several electrical companies were
convicted and sentenced to jail for conspiring to fix the prices of heavy electrical
equipment. Their defense counsel argued that they sought to rationalize a chaotic
pricing situation.* **What is your evaluation of the action of these executives?**
        Strongly Approve   Approve   Undecided   Disapprove   Strongly Disapprove

2. *Saxon is a sales representative of Ajax Tool Company. Saxon has been instructed
by Maynard,Vice President of Sales, to adopt a sales policy Saxon considers
unethical. Maynard and Saxon have discussed the policy at length and it is apparent
Maynard thinks the policy is quite ethical. Maynard orders Saxon to follow the policy,
and Saxon reluctantly does so.* **What is your opinion of Saxon's actions?**
        Strongly Approve   Approve   Undecided   Disapprove   Strongly Disapprove

3. *Stone, a member of the Board of Directors of Scott Electronic Corp., has just
learned that the company is about to announce a 2-for-1 stock split and an increase
in the dividends. Stone personally is on the brink of bankruptcy. A quick gain of a few
thousand dollars can save Stone from economic and social ruin. Stone decides to take
advantage of this information and purchases stocks now to sell back in a few days for
a profit.* **What is your opinion of Stone's actions?**
        Strongly Approve   Approve   Undecided   Disapprove   Strongly Disapprove

4. *Chuckwell sells used cars for an Auto Company. Although Chuckwell feels that the cars sold are reasonably priced, in the sales talk Chuckwell is forced to match the extravagant claims and tactics of competitors. The company engages in such practices as setting back the speedometers, hiding major defects, and putting pressure on prospects to close a deal on their first visit. Chuckwell knows that the company could not survive without such practices. Although, Chuckwell disagrees with such practices, nevertheless, Chuckwell follows these practices.* **What is your opinion of Chuckwell's actions?**

   Strongly Approve Approve Undecided Disapprove Strongly Disapprove

5. *The Reed Engineering Firm faces a very competitive situation in bidding for a large contract to construct a new store for a large discount chain. Inasmuch as the firm is seriously in need of the work, Pennings, a partner in the firm, suggests that Reed submit a bid which will certainly be low, and then make its profit on the use of inferior materials. Pennings is certain this can be done without arousing the suspicion of building inspectors. Pennings argues that any firm which is awarded the contract will have to do that since the bidding will be so competitive. Reed, senior partner, agrees, stating that it is not an infrequent practice anyway.* **What is your opinion of Penning's actions?**

   Strongly Approve Approve Undecided Disapprove Strongly Disapprove

6. *BeeBee is a sales person for Sweet Soap Company. With commissions, BeeBee's salary is $36,000 per year. BeeBee usually supplements this to the extent of about $1,800 per year by charging certain unauthorized personal expenses against the expense account. BeeBee feels that this is a common practice in the company; and if everybody is doing it, BeeBee should do it also.* **What is your opinion of BeeBee's actions?**

   Strongly Approve Approve Undecided Disapprove Strongly Disapprove

7. *Shaw, Treasurer of Lloyd Enterprises, is about to retire and contemplates recommending one of two assistants for promotion to treasurer. Shaw is sure that the recommendation will be accepted, but also knows that the assistant not recommended will find his/her promotion opportunities seriously limited. One of the assistants, Musta, seems most qualified for the new assignment, but the other assistant, Perwiz, is related to the president of Lloyd's biggest customer. Though Shaw hates to do it, Shaw recommends Perwiz for the job because the relationship with the customer will help Lloyd's.* **What is your opinion of Shaw's actions?**

   Strongly Approve Approve Undecided Disapprove Strongly Disapprove

8. *Kraft, editor of the Daily News is troubled. Kraft has just received a visit from Cramer, a public relations executive with the Aztec Department Store. Aztec is a big advertiser in the Daily News, and its continued purchase of advertising space is very important to the paper. Recently, Aztec sold a large quantity of appliances which proved to be defective, and refused to exchange the merchandise for better quality products. The Daily News at the present time is running a series on local business firms. Cramer wants to be sure that a story on the Aztec will contain no mention of this unfortunate occurrence. Kraft is troubled; but in order not to offend this*

important advertiser, Kraft agrees not to mention the sale of defective appliances.
What is your opinion of Kraft's actions?
    Strongly Approve   Approve   Undecided   Disapprove   Strongly Disapprove

9. *Schall, a Public Accountant, has been called in to audit the books of the Lakewood Trucking Company in anticipation of a public sale of stock. In the course of the audit, Schall discovered an item that is puzzling: a $20,000 advertising expense paid to a Chicago Advertising Company. This was a one-payment expense three years ago, and no further business has been done with the Chicago firm. When questioned by Schall, Wallen, President of the Trucking Company, readily admitted this money was used as a bribe to pay a union official. "It was a question of paying up or going out of business," Wallen explained. However, due to an employee empowerment program, Wallen sees no possibility of this situation recurring and asks Schall not to mention this in the Auditor's Report. Since the firm seems well managed, Schall agrees to ignore this.* **What is your opinion of Schall's actions?**
    Strongly Approve   Approve   Undecided   Disapprove   Strongly Disapprove

10. *Piser, President of Piser Fashions Co., has heard rumors that a competitor, Sunset Fashion, is coming out with a new line of spring styles which in all likelihood will sweep the market. Piser cannot afford to wait until the new styles come out and hires Bishop, plant supervisor of Sunset. Although Bishop is not a designer, in the capacity of plant supervisor Bishop has become thoroughly familiar with the new Sunset line. It is understood that Bishop will reveal the full details of the new Sunset styles to the new employer, Piser Fashions Co.* **What is your opinion of Piser's action?**
    Strongly Approve   Approve   Undecided   Disapprove   Strongly Disapprove

11. *Sarwar is a sales person for Fare and Shear, stockbrokers. Sarwar has been instructed to recommend to customers Electric Power Co. Bonds, because the brokerage firm is carrying a heavy inventory of these bonds. Sarwar does not feel the bonds are a good investment under present circumstances; and is reluctant to recommend them. However, after some thought, Sarwar decides to follow the company directive and recommend the bonds.* **What is your opinion of Sarwar's actions?**
    Strongly Approve   Approve   Undecided   Disapprove   Strongly Disapprove

COMMENTS:_____
_____
_____
_____
_____
_____
_____.

Survey Comments from Retail Employees

1. Business ethics should always be at its highest level, no matter what the circumstances might be.
2. Honesty is still the best policy.
3. I believe in the Golden Rule.
4. Hopefully, most people are not acting this way in the real world or are they?
5. Was this a test of our ethics in this company? We are not all dumb and we are very ethical, although some of us might appear a little weird.
6. Don't be unethical about any business situation. The truth is far long better, remember the truth will set you free.
7. With competition, companies will sometimes be forced to do underhand moves as long as it isn't against the law.
8. It takes a strong person to have and apply good ethics in business. But that person can make a difference in a company and make it much better in personifying the company and its image.
9. I don't believe in deceiving customers because the end-result would be far more devastating to a company's reputation, so it's better to be up front and honest from the beginning.
10. Honesty and integrity are important in all facets of life and should be upheld even if it means losing a sale.
11. It seems like most of the questions deal with bad unethical practices.
12. Regardless of the situation, fair business practice must be followed because I believe that any unfair practice will eventually come back to ruin you and the company you work for.
13. I would not work for a company that had poor morals.
14. These questions are "no-brainers." Everyone should disapprove of them.
15. Stay honest, work honestly. It may take longer but a good company stands longer with honesty.
16. I think these people in the scenarios were crude and shiftless. I could understand some of them not having enough backbone not stand up for themselves, although they should have.
17. All of these actions are untrustworthy. Our company was not built on standards such as this.
18. In some of these situations people are put in the position of following other people's orders. It is hard to avoid them, but if possible you should do what you can to stand up for yourself.
19. If you stood on principles alone, this would have been a very easy survey to fill out but in real life situations we are faced to do things that we don't necessarily agree with.
20. In the present day all great nations have fallen. We are in these days of falling. The future is in the hands of those politically running. In this country we have lost most of our ethics of "do unto others as we would have them do unto us."
21. I do not believe in deceiving people and all these question are dealing with people who are deceiving others.

22. All of the scenarios involve unethical and dishonest situations. As an employee of this company for almost seventeen years, I have been trained to be honest and to have respect for all people and other associates.
23. Good questions but not relevant to those who are younger than twenty years of age.
24. Where did you find these names?
25. It is too bad that people are put in such situations like these. I am sure some of them felt that they would lose their jobs if they didn't do what they were told. But that still isn't right for them to do it.
26. On some of these scenarios your job demands you to be unethical!! Do you want your job and livelihood or to be ethical? which is more important? If you are told to do something by an employer that you think is not right and if you don't do it, then you may lose your job. What is your decision?
27. Whether or not you approve or disapprove of the practices and actions herein, does not always have an effect on whether or not you would or would not act in the manner stated. To most people, keeping their family provided for is more important than ethics. Who can say how you will act when it is your job, life, and/or family on the line.
28. It is easy to circle disapprove on this survey because my stomach is full, my house is paid, and my bank account is in good order. But, realistically speaking, most people are not in that situation and act differently.
29. Some of the situations needed more background and in most of the situations the only way to get ahead would be to use the same tactics as their competitors. I guess it is a dog-eat-dog world and it is the only way for these companies to survive. Although their tactics are wrong and I would not enforce them.
30. Great scenarios and great names representing individuals.
31. Some of the situations do not contain enough information to base a decision on. It is also much easier to judge what is written on a page in black and white than an actual situation.
32. Seems as though all of the people mentioned are weak in back bone and honesty.
33. Each scenario given could be put on the disapprove side. Not enough information was given in some instances and others the human factor becomes involved.
34. All these situations (scenarios) are hard to make real decision because enough facts aren't given so they could depend on the situation.
35. If I knew a little more about question number nine, then I would have marked disapprove.
36. All these people in the scenarios seem to be wheelers and dealers!!
37. It seems to me that every one of these people are going against their feelings and doing what they feel is wrong.....I don't agree with that!
38. Don't have all the facts and in most cases these people don't have many choices but to go with what they are told.
39. On paper all of these ethic controversies seem to be unethical. However, to me #10 seems to be the only smart ethical business move.

40. Please use real names like Tom, John, & Steve, etc., not Piser, Schall, and so on.
41. Some of these situations you see from the persons point of view and what you need to do in life is to survive, but doesn't make it the right thing to do in every case.
42. In scenario 11, Sarwar did not really have a choice. Whether they are good decisions or not, if management says do it, it needs to be done.
43. In most of these scenarios the employee is doing what they are suppose to do. And they don't really have a choice. So, one could put approve or disapprove on these questions.
44. In question #10, the question really should be if Bishop's actions were unethical - since he is the one betraying company loyalty.
45. Promotions based on being a relative (family), scenario six, happens all the time.
46. The question about ethnicity (C on demographics) is outdated and has no use other than to widen the gap between people - this format should not be used.
47. In most of the questions you are made to follow the company's orders and you really can't make your own judgment.
48. These are probably realistic examples which put people in compromising circumstances. Government and union interference of business cause people to make compromising decisions.
49. All the situations involve dishonesty and I believe that it is wrong to knowingly cheat or steal from anyone.
50. I have noticed the scenario from question #7 practiced in our company in the past. However, I like the new way of how promotions are taking place in our company today.
51. Some of the scenarios are just good business decisions and some of them can hurt your business in the long run. It's your own personal choice and depends on whether you can get a good night sleep with the decision you made.
52. It seems today their is too much inside activity for sales and employment promotions within companies. Also, it appears as though discrimination is becoming more common in the work place.
53. Unfortunately business and ethics do not always agree. You may feel strongly against a certain situation but your job is on the line, sometimes you may have to bite the bullet.
54. In all of these scenarios, knowing first-hand information is very important.
55. These are some tough choices from the business perspective.

VIII – Journal Publications

The results of this research from the retail data have been published through the blind peer-review process in various academic conferences and journals in the United States and abroad since ethics is a cross-cultural concern for people around the globe. The following are two brief examples of papers published from the original data and doctoral dissertation study with several coauthors: one article, entitled "Ethics and Retail Management Professionals: An Examination of Gender, Age, Education, and Experience Variables," was published in the *American Journal of Business Education* (2009, 2(3), pp. 13-26) with Frank Cavico, Timothy McCartney, and Peter DiPaolo. The second article, entitled "Socializing Retail Employees in Ethical Values: The Effectiveness of the Formal versus Informal Methods," was published in the *Journal of Business and Psychology* (2006, 21(2), pp. 261-272) with Randi L. Sims. I would like to thank my coauthors, the journal editors, and the numerous blind reviewers for their input, thoughts, recommendations, and suggestions in enhancing the articles for publication and practical application. This section of the book, as examples for graduate students, provides the premise, purpose and literature review from these two articles. The original articles along with the results, analysis, and discussions of each publication can be retrieved from the original sources which might be available through each journal's website.

Ethics and Retail Management Professionals[1]

By: Bahaudin G. Mujtaba, Frank J. Cavico, Timothy O. McCartney, and Peter T. DiPaolo, Nova Southeastern University

Abstract:
Ethical maturity and behavior are of great concern to all educators, firms, and investors, and even more so in a recession. This research surveyed managers and employees in the retail environment to measure their Personal Business Ethics Scores (PBES) to see if age, education, and management experience makes a difference in making more ethical decisions. The PBES measures personal commitment to integrity, honesty, and observance of the laws regulating current business activities. This research takes into consideration the respondents' age, management experience, and education. This study contributes to the theory of moral development as it is tested with retail managers and employees.

The results of this research suggest that while age and management experience are significant factors, higher education may also play a role in the moral development of associates and managers. Kohlberg's moral development theory is

---

[1] Source: Mujtaba, B. G., Cavico, F. J., McCartney, T. O., and DiPaolo, P. T. (June 2009). Ethics and Retail Management Professionals: An Examination of Gender, Age, Education, and Experience Variables. *American Journal of Business Education, 2(3, pp. 13-26*

supported by this research since older workers, more highly educated workers, and those with more years of management experience have a higher level of moral maturity.

Introduction to Ethics and Moral Development

Reading a newspaper, skimming through academic journal articles, listening to the radio or television, and talking to investors will quickly show that people are highly concerned about the illegal and unethical decisions of executives and managers (such as Mr. Madoff, who "ripped off" billions of dollars from investors, as well as others who may have worked at high level positions with Enron, Tyco, WorldCom, and other such firms that are accused of wrongdoing). There have been many authors and researchers who have studied ethics and the unethical behaviors of managers and students in academia, as they are concerned about "copycatting" and the deleterious influence of inappropriate behaviors by managers and senior officers of major firms (Cavico and Mujtaba; 2009; Clark, 2008; Crary, 2008; McGill, 2008; Desplaces, Melchar, Beauvais, and Bosco, 2007; Gao, 2004; Klein, Levenburg, McKendall, and Mothersell, 2007; Lawson, 2004, Cherry, Lee and Chien, 2003; Nonis and Swift, 2001; Ridley and Husband, 1998; and others). Perhaps it is greed that influences people to behave unethically; or it could be a person's education, age or lack of management experience that leads one to make ethical lapses in judgment. A key research question might be to see if age, education and management experience actually makes a difference in the ethical decision making of managers. Consequently, this current research is designed to compare the Personal Business Ethics Scores (PBES) of managers and associates in the retail industry. Building on the theory of moral development, the purpose of this study is to determine whether education, age and management experience, gained through the maturation continuum or process, are related to ethical decision making.

Moral development, according to Mujtaba (1997), is the growth of a person's ability to distinguish right from wrong, to develop a system of ethical values, and to learn to act morally. The term development refers to progressive and continuous changes from the beginning of life until the end. As the research will show, moral development occurs through the process of not only maturity, but also socialization as a person acquires an education, grows older, and obtains management experience. It is believed that science, religion, culture, standards of good and bad, and other forms of behavior in society are passed on by nurture (that is, they are learned) and not by nature. The authors believe that each individual has the ability to think about his or her own thought process, which is known as "self-awareness." It is the "self-awareness" ability which enables people to make significant advances from generation to generation (Mujtaba, 1997).

Moral character is an aspect of personality, which can structure a person's moral, ethical, and personal beliefs. In general, a person may be deemed moral when he/she behaves ethically. Moral behavior appears to be a function of one's past experience with similar situations in which a person has learned to behave morally. Social and moral potentialities may be nourished best through brain development between birth and maturity, supplemented by the process of education. Moral learning is not much different from any other form of learning. Society influences behavior of its members through education and experience as people grow older. The purposes of this study are to discern if age, education and management experience are related to the ethical maturity of respondents in the retail industry.

Age and Ethics - Moral Cognizance and Morality

Does the age of a person relate to that person's moral cognizance or moral maturity, that is, does the ability to make moral determinations based on reasoning from ethical theories and principles? The following paragraphs present some studies related to the variable of age. The studies on the age variable are of two general categories: 1) those examining the age variable with a private sector employee population, and 2) those examining the age variable with a public sector employee population.

William J. Freeman (2007) studied the cognitive moral development of managers in "knowledge management" firms with those in non-"knowledge management" firms using the DIT-1 survey instrument. One of his research variables was designed to ascertain if there was a relationship between the age of the managers and moral maturity. Freeman's age variable (Freeman, 2007, p. 61) was succinctly posited as the following research question: "Is there a relationship between age and moral maturity"? The DIT was administered to two distinct groups: one group consisted of managers in firms successfully utilizing "knowledge management" as a key performance of success; and the second group consisted of managers in a company not using "knowledge management." The "knowledge management" firm was designated by one attaining the Malcolm Baldrige National Quality Award. The demographics regarding age for both groups were basically the same. Freeman's age results revealed a correlation between age and moral maturity, but not a significant one. His ultimate finding, therefore, was that there was not a significant relationship between age and moral maturity in either "knowledge management" or non-"knowledge management" firms (Freeman, 2007, p. 92). However, Freeman noted that his results on age were "...at variance with substantial research that found age as a significant influence in moral maturity (Dahl et al., 1988; McCabe et al., 1991; McNeel, 1994; Rest 1986; Rueeger & King, 1992; Weber & Wasieleski, 2001) (Freeman, 2007, p. 107)."

Donna Galla (2006) examined the moral maturity level of adult working students who worked in the finance and accounting fields. Her age research questions (Galla, 2006, p. 36) were as follows: "Is there a relationship between the moral maturity level of finance and accounting professionals and the variable of age? In other words, is there a difference in moral maturity level, as measured by the Defining Issues Test, between finance and accounting professionals who are 35 years of age and older and finance and accounting professionals who are under 35 years of age"? Although the older group of professionals had higher moral maturity scores, "the main effect for the subject's age was not significant..." (Galla, 2006, p.52). Accordingly, Galla concluded that the age of the participants did not have any "significant effect" on their moral maturity scores (Galla, 2006, p. 52).

Chunlong Huang (2006) conducted a cross-cultural examination of the moral maturity levels of U.S. and Japanese expatriate managers in Taiwan as well as Taiwanese managers who worked for Taiwanese based multinational corporations.

His research questions (Huang, 2006, p. 7) encompassing the age of his participants were as follows: "What are the variables influencing the ethical reasoning of these managers? For example, do demographic variables (i.e. Age, Gender, and Education)...relate to moral reasoning"? His specific age hypothesis, stated in the Null form, was: "There is no relationship between age and level of ethical reasoning for managers (Huang, 2006, p. 73)." His results indicated that there was no relationship between the age and the level of ethical reasoning of the managers he surveyed (Huang, 2006). Huang, however, did discuss in his literature review several studies that found a relationship between age and morality: "In their study, McCabe et al (1991) concluded that 'age correlated positively with ethical decision-making; suggesting that maturity enhances ethical decision making (p. 958).' It is generally agreed that older individuals tend to be more ethical or possess a more strict views of moral issues than younger ones. As individuals progress through the experience of life, Kohlberg (1984a) contends, they should develop higher stages of moral cognition. A survey conducted by Ruegger and King (1992) suggested that students in the 40-plus age group were the most ethical. The findings are consistent with Allmon et al (2000) research that older students exhibit more ethical inclinations (Allmon et al., 2000; Borkowski & Ugras, 1998). Accordingly, younger people tend to be less ethical than older people (Mellahi & Guermat, 2004; Miesing & Preble, 1985) or more tolerant over a wide range of issues (Longenecker, McKinney, & Moore, 1988), as older workers had stricter interpretations of ethical standards (Serwinek, 1992) (Huang, 2006, p. 55)." Yet Huang (2006) also pointed to a study by Lynon et al in 1997 that found that age had no effect on the level of moral reasoning (p. 55).

W. Thomas Heron (2006) examined the moral development and ethical decision-making of information technology professionals. Participants were selected from multiple companies in Pennsylvania whose principal business involved the production and delivery of IT products and services. The IT sample consisted of programmers, analysts, product and service support staff, project managers, and database administrators. Heron's age research questions (Heron, 2006, p. 94) were as follows: "Is there a difference in ethical maturity level between different age groups of IT professionals? Is there a difference in the ethical maturity level, as measured by the DIT-2, between IT professionals who are less than or equal to 35 years of age and IT professionals who are over 35 years of age?? Heron's age results indicated that there was "no difference in ethical maturity level between different age groups of IT professionals (Heron, 2006, p. 143)."

Donald L. Ariail (2005) examined the values and moral development of certified public accountants in Georgia. His age research question (Ariail, 2005, p. 138) was as follows: 'Is there a difference in the moral development of CPAs of different age groups"? He divided the CPA age groups into the following categories: under 30, 30-39, 40-49, 50-59, and 60 and over. Ariail (2005) found that the age groups 40-49 and 50-59 had higher DIT moral maturity scores than the other categories, but the scores were not statistically significant, and thus he answered his age research question in the negative (pp. 198-204). Arial in his literature review pointed to studies that showed a relationship between age and morality, but conversely he related that prior studies with accountants showed no relationship between age and moral development or a negative relationship (Ariail, 2005).

Pamela K. Smith Evans (2004) investigated the ethical maturity of African-American business professionals who worked as managers and employees in the private sector as well as entrepreneurs, and who were members of the National Black Master of Business Administration organization. Among other variables, she sought to determine if age influences their ethical maturity levels. Her age research questions (Smith Evans, 2004, pp. 48-49) were as follows: "Is there a difference in ethical maturity level between different age groups of African-American business professionals? That is, is there a difference in ethical maturity, as measured by the Defining Issues Test, between African-American business professionals who are under 35 years of age and African-American business professionals who are over 35 years of age"? Smith Evans' results showed that "…there is no difference in ethical maturity level between different age groups of African-American business professionals (Smith Evans, 2004, p. 74).

Maisie E. Reid (2004) examined the cognitive moral development of health care executives working in a managed care organizational environment. Her age related research questions (Reid, 2004, p. 53) were as follows: "Is there a relationship between ethical maturity level and health care professionals' age? Specifically, is there a difference in ethical maturity level between health care professionals who are 40 years of age and over, and health care professionals below 40 years of age"? Reid distributed 550 DIT surveys to health care professionals at a large county health care hospital district in southeast Florida. Within age groups, 56% of her respondents were under 40 years of age, and 44% were 40 years of age and older. The data that Reid obtained did not show any significant difference between ethical maturity level of health care executives and their age (Reid, 2004, p.72). Reid, however, did observe that her age findings were "…inconsistent with findings of most prior DIT studies, which indicate that (moral maturity) scores advance in age and education (Brockett, Geddes, Westmoreland, & Salvatori, 1997; Elm & Nicholas, 1993; White, 1999; Wimalasiri, Pavri & Jalil, 1996) (Reid, 2004, p. 76)."

Joseph Chavez (2003) examined the moral maturity scores on Kohlberg's scale as measured by the Defining Issues Test of banking employees in southeast Florida. His survey sample consisted of 300 participants working in the banking industry. The age of the employees was one of the factors that he tested. His age research questions (Chavez, 2003, p. 44) were as follows: "Is there a relationship between moral maturity and age of banking employees? In other words, is there a difference in moral maturity level, as measured by the Defining Issues Test, between banking employees who are over 30 years of age and older and banking employees who are not yet 30 years of age"? His results indicated that "the data shows that the banking employees that are not yet 30 years and younger tend to have lower (moral maturity) P scores than banking employees who are 30 years of age and older (Chavez, 2003, p. 58). Regarding his age variable, Chavez concluded: "The common perception of being 'older and wiser' may prove correct since the results of this study show that participants older than 30 years of age made moral and ethical decisions closer to those moral philosophers with the highest degree of moral maturity (Chavez, 2003, pp. 58-59)."

Franck Aurel Hyppolite (2003) examined the ethical maturity level of public sector employees at the local government level. His sample consisted of 400 managerial, supervisory, and non-managerial employees employed by Broward County, Florida, municipalities therein, and local government agencies. Age was one of the variables he tested. His age research question (Hyppolite, 2003, p. 128) was as follows: "Is there a relationship between the ethical maturity level and the age of public sector employees"? His specific age hypothesis, stated in the Null form, was as follows: "There is no relationship between the ethical maturity level and the age of public sector employees (Hyppolite, 2003, p. 81)." This null hypothesis, however, was rejected, meaning that he in fact did find a positive relationship between age and morality in his study (Hyppolite, 2003, p. 128). Hyppolite (2003) discussed his age finding: "The fourth research question focused on relationship between the ethical maturity level and the age of public sector employees and confirmed this research analysis. This study's findings exposed that there was a significant correlation between the two variables. Hence, this research observation generated important conclusions for the study of both age and Cognitive Moral Development (CMD). The average P-score (for moral maturity) of older participants was higher than the one of younger respondents. As one matures with age, one's average P-score increases....Indeed this current research indicated age was a predictor of individual maturity level (p. 139)."

Lexine V. Arthur (2003) examined the cognitive moral development level of contracting professionals at the federal administrative agency – the General Services Administration (GSA). She sought to see if a relationship existed between age, among other variables, and the cognitive moral development of her survey population at the GSA. Arthur's age related research questions (Arthur, 2003, p. 39) were as follows: "Is there a relationship between ethical maturity and age of the contracting professional? As measured by the Defining Issues Test, is there a difference in ethical maturity between contracting professionals and the age of the contracting professionals."? She found that there was a relationship but not a statistically "significant" one; and thus she concluded that there was no significant relationship between the age of the contracting professionals and their level of moral maturity (Arthur, 2003, pp. 68-69).

Sandra E. Ford Mobley (2002) examined the moral development level of managerial employees of the state of Virginia. Age was one of her variables. Her age research questions (Mobley, 2002, pp. 51-52) were as follows: "Is there a relationship between the ethical maturity level and public sector managers' age? In other words, as measured by Rest's DIT, is there a difference in ethical maturity level between public sector managers who are 45 years of age and over and public sector managers below 45 years of age." Although her data indicated that the 45 and older category had higher moral maturity scores, the difference was not statistically significant, and thus she answered the age research question in the negative (Mobley, 2002).

Carol Cannon (2001) examined the moral reasoning abilities of 226 adult working learners at a private university in the southwestern part of the United States. Age was one of the variables that she tested. Her age premise was as follows: "Higher levels of moral development, as measured by the DIT, are significantly related to higher levels of chronological age for working adult learners (Cannon, 2001, p. 166)." Furthermore, she posited: "If age is related to differences in moral development, with adults evidencing continuing development, then it is anticipated that the work adult learners in the present study, aged 36 or greater, will exhibit a higher moral development level than working adults younger than 36 (Cannon, 2001, p. 195)." Cannon's results "...revealed that DIT scores for working adults, equal to or over the age of 36, were significantly higher... than DIT mean scores of working adults younger than 36 years...(Cannon, 2001, p. 195)." Cannon's review of the age and moral cognizance literature overall corroborated her findings and conclusion. She related that "in a ten-year, interdisciplinary, longitudinal study examining factors of moral development, Rest (1986) discovered consistent gains in moral judgment with increasing chronological age. Thoma (1985) found further empirical support for age as a predictor or moral development in a meta-analysis of multidisciplinary ethics studies. Ford and Richardson (1994) reviewed eight moral development studies of which five found no significant relationship between age and moral development, and three reported significant, but contradictory results. Borkowski and Ugras (1998) further observed a positive relationship between chronological age and moral development in a meta-analysis of empirical studies ranging from 1985 through 1994. Studies specifically in accounting, on the other hand, tend to provide conflicting evidence to the relation of chronological age and moral development (Enyon, Throley, Hill, & Stevens, 1997; Ponemon, 1990; Shaub, 1994). Overall, however, these studies suggest that attitudes/behavior appear to become more ethical with age, thereby providing empirical support for Kohlberg's CMD theory that individuals will increase in moral development as they mature (Cannon, 2001, p. 166)."

Kohlberg's Cognitive Moral Development theory posits that as a person increases in age, his or her capability and level of moral reasoning should concomitantly and progressively increase too. Furthermore, as a person increases in age, so does the complexity of the moral questions that a person will confront; and accordingly moral reasoning *should* increase with age. So, does age in fact relate to morality in the sense of moral cognizance or moral maturity? The evidence obtained from the above studies, as well as their review of the age and morality literature, is plainly mixed. Seven of the aforementioned studies found that there was a relationship between age and moral maturity, though not necessarily a statistically significant one; whereas five studies found there was no relationship between age and moral maturity. Perhaps age in combination with education would demonstrate a stronger link to moral maturity than between "mere" age and moral maturity (Mobley, 2002, p. 74; Mujtaba, 1996, p. 24). In fact, Heron (2006) pointed to one study that reported that 38% of the variance in the Defining Issues Test (moral cognizance) scores can be explained by the variables of age *and* education (p. 87). Therefore, the study for this article focused on the following hypothesis:

> *Null Hypothesis I - Individuals who are 25 years of age or younger will have Personal Business Ethics Scores (PBES) that are equivalent to or greater than those individuals who are 26 years of age or older.*

Management Experience and Ethics – Moral Cognizance and Morality

Is there a relationship between one's position and tenure or experience as a manager and one's level of moral maturity? Kennedy noted that an important issue confronting business leadership and ethics studies is whether "...there may be a deficiency in moral development of business leaders, especially in principled reasoning and emphatic concern" (Kennedy, 2003, p. 51).

Huang (2006) conducted a cross-cultural examination of the moral maturity levels of U.S. and Japanese expatriate managers in Taiwan as well as Taiwanese managers who worked for Taiwanese based multinational corporations. He sought to determine if there was a relationship between a manager's ethical reasoning ability and his or her years of experience as an expatriate employee (Huang, 2006, pp. 79-80). He found that no such relationship existed for any of his managerial groups (Huang, 2006, pp. 106-108). He also found that no significant relationship existed in the ethical reasoning abilities of the managers based on their level of education (Huang, 2006, p. 94).

Kennedy (2003) examined the cognitive moral development of "leaders," which encompassed executives, managers, and administrators. He sampled "leaders" in a bank, an insurance company, a computer company, a telephone company, and a military command. One of his variables dealt with the experience of the individual leader in the organization. His experience research question (Kennedy, 2003, p. 74) was as follows: "Is there a difference in moral judgment by the individual's level of experience in the organization"? His results indicated that the experience held by an organizational leader did not relate positively to the leader's moral judgment level (Kennedy, 2003, p. 75).

Hyppolite (2003) examined the ethical maturity level of public sector employees at the local government level. His sample consisted of 400 managerial, supervisory, and non-managerial employees employed by Broward County, Florida, municipalities therein, and local government agencies. He performed a comparative analysis of managers and non-managers regarding the variable of education. Specifically, he sought to ascertain whether a relationship existed between the managers' as well as the non-managers' level of education and their ethical maturity and moral reasoning (Hyppolite, 2003, p. 81-82). He also sought to determine if such a relationship existed between ethical maturity and the rank or position one held in the organization (Hyppolite, 2003, p. 82). Although Hyppolite stated that Rest found that education is the strongest predictor of Cognitive Moral Development, he nevertheless found that there was neither a positive relationship between cognitive moral development and education for managers nor non-managers (Hyppolite, 2003, pp. 137-38). He also found that there was not a positive relationship between the rank and position variables and moral maturity (Hyppolite, 2003, p. 139).

Cannon (2001) examined the moral reasoning abilities of 226 adult working learners at a private university in the southwestern part of the United States. Work experience was one of the variables that she tested. Her work experience research premise was that higher levels of work experience are significantly related to levels of moral development, as measured by the Defining Issues Test, for the adult working learner (Cannon, 2001, p. 168). Cannon (2001) noted that Rest considered work experience to be a positive cognitive moral development variable. In her research, Cannon (2001) did find a "slightly higher" DIT score for working adults with 14 years or more of work experience, but not a significantly higher score, and thus she answered her research question in the negative and accordingly concluded that work experience does not predict moral development based on her study (pp. 198-99). She also noted that the relationship between work experience and moral development is not well documented in the literature (Cannon, 2001, p. 198).

Therefore, the study for this article focused on the following hypothesis:

> *Null Hypothesis II - Individuals who have five or more years of management experience will have Personal Business Ethics Scores that are equivalent to or greater than individuals who do not have any management experience at all.*

Education and Ethics - Moral Cognizance and Morality

Is there a relationship between education and higher levels of moral development and reasoning? Do years of education, particularly higher education, emerge as a predictor of ethical reasoning and moral development? Many studies report a strong, positive, and predictive relationship between education and ethics, and especially with Kohlberg's levels of Cognitive Moral Development as ascertained by Rest's Defining Issues Test (Freeman, 2007).

Freeman (2007) studied the cognitive moral development of managers in "knowledge management" firms with those in non-"knowledge management" firms using the DIT-1 survey instrument. One of his research questions was designed to ascertain if there was a relationship between the education level of the managers and moral maturity. Specifically, his education research question (Freeman, 2007, p. 62) was as follows: "Is there a relationship between highest level of formal education attained and moral maturity"? He had several education hypotheses dealing with education, encompassing vocational and technical school, high school, to college, graduate school, and professional school education that he used to test his education research question (Freeman, 2007, pp. 62-65). Freeman's research indicated that there was a positive significant relationship between all these levels of education and moral maturity (Freeman, 2007, pp. 98, 108).

Smith Evans (2004) investigated the ethical maturity of African-American business professionals who worked as managers and employees in the private sector as well as entrepreneurs, and who were members of the National Black Master of Business Administration organization. Among other variables, she sought to determine if level of education influenced their ethical maturity levels. Her education research questions (Smith Evans, 2004, p.50) are as follows: "Is there a difference in ethical maturity level between different groups of formally educated African-American business professionals? That is, is there a difference in ethical maturity, as measured by the Defining Issues Test, between African=American business professionals who have completed one to four years of formal undergraduate education and African-American business professionals who have completed one to two years of formal graduate education"? Her study indicated that there was a difference in the ethical maturity level between groups of formally educated African-American business professionals (Smith Evans, 2004, p. 76). She reported that "the statistical evidence...indicated formal education for African-American business professionals, as measured by the DIT, results in increased levels of cognitive moral development (CMD)" (Smith Evans, 2004, p. 81). Smith Evans (2004) concluded that her research substantiated Rest's assertion that "education is the greatest predictor of ethical maturity" (p. 81).

Kennedy (2003) examined the cognitive moral development of "leaders," which encompassed executives, managers, and administrators. He sampled "leaders" in a bank, an insurance company, a computer company, a telephone company, and a military command. He ended up with 147 usable DIT-2 surveys. His education research question (Kennedy, 2003, p. 52) was as follows: "Is there a difference in moral judgment by the individual's level of education"? He found that there is a positive difference in moral judgment by educational level of the leaders he surveyed (Kennedy, 2003, pp. 71-72). He also demonstrated that there was a positive significant relationship between the amount of ethics training received by the leaders and their moral maturity levels (Kennedy, 2003, pp. 72-73). Kennedy related that according to Rest, "...people who develop in moral judgment are those who love to learn, seek new challenges, enjoy intellectually stimulating environments, are reflective, make plans, set goals, take risks, see themselves in the larger social contexts of history, institutions and broad cultural trends, and take responsibility for themselves and their environment" (Kennedy, 2003, p. 71).

Mobley (2002) examined the moral development level of managerial employees of the state of Virginia. Her education research questions (Mobley, 2002, p. 51) were as follows: "Is there a relationship between ethical maturity level and public sector managers' level of education? In other words, as measured by Rest's Defining Issues Test (DIT), is there a difference in ethical maturity level between public sector managers with post-secondary degrees and public sector managers without post-secondary degrees"? She explained that the "P" score in Rest's formulation "...is the representation of the degree to which a person's thinking resembles that of moral philosophers" (Mobley, 2002, p. 63). Her results indicated that there was indeed a relationship between education and moral maturity, and in fact, based on her review of the literature and her own research results, Mobley (2002) concluded that "...among the demographic variables, education is by far the most powerfully associated with DIT scores" (p. 71).

The study for this article focused on the following hypothesis:

Null Hypothesis III - Individuals who have four or more years of formal college education will have Personal Business Ethics Scores that are equivalent to or greater than individuals who do not have any formal college education.

For the analysis, results, and discussions, please see the actual journal article as follows:

- Mujtaba, B. G., Cavico, F. J., McCartney, T. O., and DiPaolo, P. T. (June 2009). Ethics and Retail Management Professionals: An Examination of Gender, Age, Education, and Experience Variables. *American Journal of Business Education, 2(3).pp. 13-26*

Conclusions

This research was designed to compare the Personal Business Ethics Scores (PBES) of associates who are under 26 years of age and have no management experience, with the Personal Business Ethics Scores of managers who are at least 26 years of age and have six or more years of management experience in the retail industry. The purpose was to determine whether education, age, and management experience, gained through the maturation continuum or process, are related to ethical decision making. This research has concluded that age and management are significant factors in the moral development of respondents. While the education variable was not a significant factor, those with a college degree did have a higher score than respondents who did not have a college degree. So, it can be suggested that education, age and management experience can increase a person's level of ethical maturity in the workplace. Future researchers, therefore, should collect more data from respondents with a college degree to see how their scores compare with those without a college degree.

Socializing Retail Employees in Ethical Values[2]

By: Bahaudin G. Mujtaba and Randi L. Sims, Nova Southeastern University

Abstract:
The purpose of this study was to test the effectiveness of an informal socialization process for reported employee attitudes towards unethical behavior within a large retail organization. This study compares the reported ethical attitudes of full-time employees who were socialized using an informal approach, to the reported ethical attitudes of their managers who were socialized using a formal approach. The results indicate that the informal approach to ethical socialization was not as effective as the formal approach to ethical socialization. Employees were more accepting of unethical behavior than were their managers. Implications are discussed and recommendations provided.

Introduction

Individuals have their own set of values that guide their personal and professional decisions. People form these values, in part, during the socialization process. Socialization is defined as the process by which people learn the ways of a culture or society so they can effectively function within it (Rice, 1995). In early childhood, the socialization process helps children learn the patterns of behavior expected by their family and by the educational system they become a part of when they enroll in school. Children are taught the ways, values, and ethical perspectives of their society through contact with already socialized members, initially family members and then others such as educators, peers, and media personalities. Through socialization and over time, one's understanding of right and wrong are created and formed. However, the socialization process does not end in childhood. Adults begin the socialization process all over again every time they accept new employment. "Organizational socialization is often identified as the primary process by which people adapt to new jobs and organizational roles" (Chao, O'Leary-Kelly, Wolf, Klein, & Gardner, 1994, p. 730). As with each family and school, every organization has a standard expectation of behavior for its members. Within the organization, socialization ensures that new employees learn the accepted ways of responding to each situation and the expected ways of working with others. "To perform effectively, newcomers need information that enables them to [do] their job, and information that will help them understand the behavioral patterns of the people with whom they work" (Comer, 1989, p. 84). An effective organizational socialization process leads to an alignment between the employee's values and the organization's values (Cable & Parsons, 2001). "The stability and productivity of any organization depend in large

---

[2]*Source*: Mujtaba, B. and Sims, R. L., (December 2006). Socializing Retail Employees in Ethical Values: The Effectiveness of the Formal versus Informal Methods. *Journal of Business and Psychology*, 21(2), pp. 261-272.

measure on the way newcomers to various organizational positions come to carry out their tasks" (Van Maanen, 1978, p. 20).

If socialization was a perfect process, children and adults alike would never stray from the expected behavior patterns established by society and organizations. In addition, the expected modes of behavior would be consistent from situation to situation. This is far from reality, however. Instead, the variations in expected behaviors from one situation to the next and from one organization to another often lead to confusion and contradictory and unethical behavior (see also Fritz, Arnett, & Conkel, 1999; Siegel, Agrawal, & Rigsby, 1997). Yet, when there is work behavior agreement between the employee and his/her supervisor or manager, employee job satisfaction was increased and conflict decreased (Feldman, 1976). Thus, the importance of organizational socialization techniques becomes an important area of study.

Much of the study of organizational socialization focuses on employee outcomes like satisfaction, commitment, and turnover. Few studies actually test socialization effectiveness (Anakwe & Greenhaus, 1999). This study, specifically, considers the effectiveness of socialization related to unethical behavior, considered a neglected area of study by Dose (1997). For socialization to be effective, employee values should change to match those of the organization. Kraimer's (1997) research concluded that when work value congruence between employee and employer is low, the employee "may engage in detrimental behaviors" (p. 425). Other research has found that low value congruence (ethical fit) is related to increases in reported feelings of discomfort and intrapersonal role conflict (Sims & Keon, 2000) and increases in reported intentions to quit (Kraimer, 1997; Sims & Kroeck, 1994). "The individual's work values must match the organization's work values in order for knowledge acquisition to lead to positive attitudes and behaviors" (Kraimer, 1997, p. 442). Although unlikely across large numbers of new hires, it is also possible for this match to already exist because of a superior recruitment process where only applicants who share the organization's values are selected for employment. The current study does not consider this circumstance.

For the remaining literature, analysis, results, and discussions, please see the actual journal article as follows:

- Mujtaba, B. and Sims, R. L., (December 2006). Socializing Retail Employees in Ethical Values: The Effectiveness of the Formal versus Informal Methods. *Journal of Business and Psychology,* Volume 21(2), pp. 261-272. Available at: http://www.springerlink.com/content/18r533570827151h/

Conclusion

The results of this study indicate that the informal socialization of employees for ethical business issues is less effective than the formal approach of orientation and training. Managers reported higher levels of disapproval for the unethical behaviors described in the vignettes of the PBES than did the non-managers in the sample. The retail organization represented in this study takes great strides to ensure that managers are well-trained to make positive ethical decisions. As with many retail organizations, this company is quite centralized. Employees are expected to follow clearly established rules and procedures. Any decisions to make exceptions are left to the management staff. In this way, perhaps the corporate headquarters feels as if ensuring high ethical values of the management staff is sufficient to ensure high ethical decisions since only management is authorized to make decisions. However, corporate may be shortsighted in this thinking.

While non-managers may not be authorized to make exceptions to rules and procedures, there are opportunities for employees to behave in an unethical manner. These opportunities come in the treatment of customers and co-workers, in the display of work ethic, and in opportunities of employee theft.

Given the opportunity for employees to behave in an unethical manner in the workplace, corporate should rethink the decision to exclude non-management employees from the ethical training and workshops already established. While the costs of these programs will increase with increased enrollment, it is possible to lessen these costs by using local staff in each store or district. For example, each store has already been staffed with a professional trainer who works with employees to ensure they have the job skills to be successful in their assigned position. The addition of ethical training to the already established programs is one possibility. As a non-management person, the trainer may have a better rapport with the employees who may feel more comfortable approaching someone who is not their supervisor. "Newcomers seem to prefer socialization by peers. When they need someone to supply them with information, they consider people at their own level as more approachable because they do not want the supervisor to know [their] weaknesses" (Comer, 1989, 85).

As with many retail operations, there are times of the year when there are fewer new hires. This means that the trainer has more time available to work with existing employees to cover ethical issues. Of course, as a non-management employee, store trainers may not have yet received training in ethical issues. This must be the first step.

IX - Index

Author Biography

Bahaudin G. Mujtaba is an Associate Professor of Management, Human Resources and International Management. As a corporate manager and trainer, he has worked in management development, human resources, and improvement systems departments. His consulting work is in the areas of customer service, ethics training, diversity management, and change management. Bahaudin worked in the retail environment for sixteen years as a part-time associate, full-time employee, assistant department manager, department manager, management development specialist, senior training specialist, and an internal coach and consultant for executives.

Bahaudin has been teaching for about fifteen years now. In the years 2003-2005, he was the Director of Institutional Relations, Planning, and Accreditation for Nova Southeastern University at the H. Wayne Huizenga School of Business and Entrepreneurship in Fort Lauderdale, Florida. As a director, he was responsible for the planning of accreditation reviews for all Huizenga School's academic programs. Bahaudin's areas of research include ethics, management, and cross-cultural management practices. He has written and coauthored over fifteen books. Some of Bahaudin's books include the following:

1. Cavico, F. J. & Mujtaba, B. G. (2009). *Business Ethics: The Moral Foundation of Leadership, Management, and Entrepreneurship (2nd edition).* Pearson Custom Publications. Boston, USA.
2. Mujtaba, B. G. (2008). *Coaching and Performance Management: Developing and Inspiring Leaders.* ILEAD Academy Publications; Davie, Florida, USA.
3. Cavico, F. & Mujtaba, B. G., (2008). *Legal Challenges for the Global Manager and Entrepreneur.* Kendal Hunt Publishing Company. United States.
4. Cavico, F. & Mujtaba, B. G., (2008). *Business Law for the Entrepreneur and Manager.* ILEAD Academy Publications; Davie, Florida, USA. ISBN: 978-0-9774-2115-2.
5. Mujtaba, B. G. and Scharff, M. M. (2007). *Earning a Doctorate Degree in the 21st Century: Challenges and Joys.* ILEAD Academy Publications; Florida, USA.
6. Mujtaba, B. G. (2007). *Cross Cultural Management and Negotiation Practices.* ILEAD Academy Publications; Florida, United States. ISBN: 978-0-9774211-2-1.
7. Mujtaba, B. G. (2007). *Workplace Diversity Management: Challenges, Competencies and Strategies.* Llumina Press; Davie, Florida; United States.
8. Mujtaba, B. G. (2007). *AFGHANISTAN: Realities of war and rebuilding (2nd edition).* ILEAD Academy, LLC, Davie, Florida; United States.
9. Mujtaba, B. G. and McCartney, T. (2007). *Managing Workplace Stress and Conflict amid Change.* Llumina Press, Coral Springs, Florida, USA. ISBN: 1-59526-414-0.
10. Mujtaba, Bahaudin G. (2007). *The ethics of management and leadership in Afghanistan (2nd edition).* ILEAD Academy. ISBN: 978-0-9774211-0-7. Davie, Florida USA.
11. Mujtaba, B. G. (2007). *Mentoring Diverse Professionals (2nd edition).* Llumina Press.
12. Mujtaba, B. G. and Preziosi, R. C. (2006). *Adult Education in Academia: Recruiting and Retaining Extraordinary Facilitators of learning.* 2nd Edition. Information Age Publishing. Greenwich, Connecticut.
13. Mujtaba, B. G. (2006). *Cross Cultural Change Management.* Llumina Press, Tamarac, Florida.
14. Mujtaba, G. B. (2006). *Privatization and Market-Based Leadership in Developing Economies: Capacity Building in Afghanistan.* Llumina Press and Publications, Tamarac, Florida.
15. Mujtaba, B. G. and Cavico, F. J., (2006). *Age Discrimination in Employment: Cross Cultural Comparison and Management Strategies.* BookSurge. ISBN: 1-4196-1587-4.

Bahaudin can be reached through email at: mujtaba@nova.edu

The Man in the Glass, Poem by Dale Wimbrow

When you get what you want in your struggle for self
      And the world makes you king for a day,
Just go to a mirror and look at yourself
      And see what THAT man has to say.

For it isn't your father or mother or wife
      Whose judgment upon you must pass;
The fellow whose verdict counts most in your life
      Is the one staring back from the glass.

Some people may think you a straight-shootin' chum
      And call you a wonderful guy,
But the man in the glass says you're only a bum
      If you can't look him straight in the eye.

He's the fellow to please, never mind all the rest,
      For he's with you clear up to the end.
And you've passed your most dangerous, difficult test
      If the man in the glass is your friend.

You may fool the whole world down the pathway of life
      And get pats on your back as you pass,
But your final reward will be heartaches and tears
      If you've cheated the man in the glass.

www.ingramcontent.com/pod-product-compliance
Lightning Source LLC
Chambersburg PA
CBHW031946190326
41519CB00007B/680